UMPIRE

DIARY

SAMUEL BARRETT

UMPIRE DIARY

Copyright © 2024 Samuel Barrett

Typesetting, Book Layout, Editing and by Enger Lanier Taylor for In Due Season Publishing

Published By: In Due Season Publishing ®
                Huntsville, Alabama
                indueseasonpublishing@gmail.com

ISBN-13: 978-1-970057-40-9
ISBN-10: 1-970057-40-8

Limits of Liability and Disclaimer of Warranty

Printed in the United States of America

SAMUEL BARRETT

TABLE OF CONTENTS

ACKNOWLEDGMENTS   6

INTRODUCTION   12

Diary Dates

December 31, 2020 to AUGUST 8, 2021

EJECTION REPORTS   146

CHARACTER LIST   151

Q&A   160

CONCLUSION   177

BIOGRAPHY   184

UMPIRE DIARY

ACKNOWLEDGMENTS

There are so many people to whom I owe my gratitude for helping me write this book. Some have molded me into the person I am today. Some have developed my skills as an umpire. And some, you could say, gave me lemons to turn into lemonade, just as Wally Amos described in his book, *Man With No Name: Turn Lemons Into Lemonade.*

Biologically, no person becomes anything without their parents. I am no exception. My parents have never given up on me, even when it would have been easy for them to accept less from me. When I was first diagnosed with autism spectrum disorder as a child, the doctors told my mother that I would never speak to her. No mother wants to hear such a limiting blanket statement about what her child will be incapable of, and mine decided that what she heard was not good enough. Our access to excellent early intervention in Decatur, Alabama, helped me eventually speak to her. The doctors later qualified their statement by saying she would be the only person I would ever talk to. Of course, today, you can see that this did not last either. However, the experts maintained that I would never be able to operate in a standard classroom setting and would need to enroll in special education classes. I imagine my mother was full of questions: Would I ever move out on my own? Would I ever drive a car? Would I ever hold down a job? Would I ever make friends? These concerns have only begun to be disproven in recent years. Still, the groundwork was laid early in my life to ensure I could achieve these things, thanks to my family's endless love and perseverance at a time when I was incapable of such feelings for myself. Only a genuinely selfless soul would be willing to shift their attention away from themselves to such a degree as my parents did. My parents certainly are not the only ones who have made such sacrifices, but among the friends, I gained during and since high school, I'd bet that none of their parents had to do so to the extent mine did just to get me to the point where I could start kindergarten on time with my sister Anna Grace and other peers our age. The massive efforts made by my family have surely made my academic achievements, social interactions, and outgoing endeavors, such as going to umpire school and the Expedition League, as well as writing this book (and likely more in the future), very rewarding in my family's eyes.

Just as my immediate family made sacrifices for me, my grandparents have shown me an equal amount of love. I have two grandparents on my father's side who live in Suwanee, Georgia, and look for any opportunity to support their children and grandchildren. On my mother's side, my grandfather has been my most relatable relative, and my Nana, who is not biologically related to me and my sister but nonetheless claims us as her grandchildren, enjoys showing her love whenever she can. My biological maternal grandmother died in October 2009, but my sister and I knew her well enough to look forward to seeing her whenever we could.

Just as my family helped me develop, my start in baseball in eighth grade provided me with a plethora of friends who, while they initially scared me since I viewed them as cooler and better than me, took me under their wing and allowed me to not only be myself but grow into who I was. They and our coaches think I helped them with everyday operations and creating a positive atmosphere, but they have no idea how much they poured into me without even realizing it. The things I did for them were just for a day or a season. Their impact broke my shell and gave me the confidence to believe that life is better outside the shell, which has lasted far longer than a game, season, or tenure. Some of these friends include Riley Rutledge, Andrew Valero, Slade Gorman, Peyton Burton, Mason Davis, Jay Kehoe, Brayden Pelkey, Gage Tillery, Jeremy Thorn, Noah Butler, Nick Nason, DJ Rias, Tommy Vickers, and, of course, Tucker Melton, whom I will mention a couple of times. I'm sure I've forgotten some names, so I'll just have to beg their forgiveness.

These relationships prepared me to develop similar connections with peers at umpire school, who had similar impacts in shorter time spans. Among these friends are Derek Stevenson, Kolten Black, Alex Schumaker, Xavier Wood, Marv Gomez, Jeff Wallace, Matt Youkhanna, Mike MacStudy, Frank Jones, Ryan Haswell, ArRee Bateman, and plenty of others listed in the character list. I also met a fellow Alabamian during my second time through umpire school in 2022 named Adam Luck, who is also fantastic. He knows his stuff, not only on the field but also about how much more umpires could be paid than they are. He got to see me call a flawless plate game during Game 1 of the first round of my high school postseason at Munford High School since he lived not too far from there at the time, and he recalled hearing some fans say they would see me in the big leagues one day. In the Expedition League, Jake Al-Mazroa, my first-ever crew partner, will always be remembered by me, and I imagine I will be remembered by him as well. In the span of two weeks, we had some eventful games and days, but we stuck through it together. Tristyn Jones, my second crew partner and the one I was with for most of the season deserves and receives my everlasting appreciation for guiding me through a tumultuous summer. I have no idea how it would have turned out had I not been moved to his crew. No longer was I confined to a silent hotel room until game time or eating either Papa John's Pizza or our postgame meal with someone who was just as new to this as I was. We went out and explored, which is not in my nature but something I do desire. There may not be one single person in this book or related to my umpire career who deserves my acknowledgment more than Tristyn.

Another valuable acknowledgment goes to a practical acknowledgment in terms of this book. Gary Livacari, who has written and/or assisted with the writing of at least four baseball books, including *Paul Pryor In His Own Words: The Life and Times of a 20-Year Major League Umpire*, offered to proofread and copyedit any portions of this book that I emailed to him. He assured me that I did not have to use all of his suggestions, as he understood this was my project and should be how I wanted it. This demeanor immediately assured me that I was talking to someone I would benefit from having edited my writing. While I did not have the day-by-day accounts edited since I wanted to keep those entries' originality and authenticity, he gave me plenty of changes to consider for my introduction and conclusion. I look forward to having him help me with future books.

If you like the cover art, look no further than the steady hand and eye of photographer Wes Roberts. He took my senior pictures back when I was in high school, and we agreed to do a photo shoot to get some good pictures for the cover. I think his work blends seamlessly with the cover design, so if you were drawn to the look of this book or you "judged a book by its cover," Wes Roberts made this book pop out to you.

To Enger Lanier Taylor with In Due Season Publishing, I thank you for accepting this project and helping to make this story of mine come alive for many others to see. I was skeptical about where I wanted to take this manuscript to get published, and when I investigated In Due Season, I felt like this was the fit, and as you can now see, it was. Her dedication to what she does is evident by what you will see on these pages, the emails I received at midnight, and text messages at seven a.m. Sometimes, I would get three or four emails from In Due Season in one day to accomplish as much as possible. I'm so glad to say that all that has paid off in the physical form, where long after I depart this Earth, my words will remain to breathe my legacy to all who turn these pages. What more can someone ask than that?

The last acknowledgment goes to the Almighty. The Lord, our God, provided all these other people in my life and, during the times of this book, opened the opportunities that I would later write about, and had long since gotten me to a point where I would be capable of considering putting together a project such as this book. When I pray to Him for the life He can give me, I tell Him the same thing Steve Harvey says he prayed when he was homeless: "If you let me get there, I'll tell everybody it was You." Well, here I am, and it was God. Sure, you can write a book without Him, but chances are those who say that are either not writing a book or not getting through the things He carried me through.

To anyone I neglected to mention, I promise it is not on purpose, and you are also greatly appreciated.

INTRODUCTION

The idea for this book came from several different sources. The most significant was Jim Bouton's groundbreaking bestseller, *Ball Four*. In case you haven't read it, Bouton depicts the day-to-day life of a Major League Baseball player during a season in great detail. The book is very telling because Bouton experienced in one season many things a professional athlete does throughout a career: the thrill and relief of making the big league club out of spring training, the endless traveling from city to city, the daily, carefree baseball banter engaged in between players, coaches, and managers, and the stressful, yet necessary, dealings with front office executives. He knew the heartbreak and stress of being demoted to the minor leagues mid-season - almost unexpectedly - and then the joy of being promoted back to the majors. He faced the optimism and anxiety of being traded, which allowed him to experience firsthand the difference between playing on a poor team versus a contender. This was real-life baseball written from an insider's point of view.

I've often glanced through *Ball Four* when I'm curious about recalling an episode from the book. Recently, after hearing the idea from a family friend, I began to think, "Well, I spent a few months in a league that conducted itself like professional baseball. Maybe I could compile all the blog posts I wrote for my family and friends back home and combine them into a book. Maybe others would enjoy reading about my own everyday experiences in baseball." Some of this may resemble Anne Frank's "The Diary of a Young Girl" more than "Ball Four." If you've chosen to buy my book, I guess I was right: the interest is there, and I greatly appreciate you taking the time to read it.

A month before I went to Ormond Beach, Florida, to attend the Wendelstedt Umpire School for the first time, I decided to start an online blog. I sought an easy way to share my experiences with everyone back home. That way, I wouldn't have to retell my stories to everyone individually. But before I get into all that, let me briefly introduce myself through a statement that will neatly transition into the school details...

I haven't been a baseball fan all my life, but rather for a little less than half of it. I am 23 years old now and turned 20 years old on Election Day 2020, not long before I started the blog. I had an on-and-off enjoyment of baseball in my backyard as I grew up, but I didn't develop the level of interest that would progress into what it is now until I was 12. Now, years later, and given my work ethic, my understanding of the game's intricacies, my knowledge of the game's history, my willingness to learn, and my intense interest in baseball that I later developed, I firmly believe that if I had started playing earlier in my life, I would have become an elite player. I believe I would have been given the opportunity to sign with a Division-1 college out of high school. Of course, I may never know exactly how far I could have gone had my life taken that route - a concept I'm totally at peace with - but it's still one I enjoy imagining on occasion.

I know all this might sound a bit like bragging, but I can assure you I'm not an arrogant guy. Rather, I'm just a thinking guy - someone who enjoys speculating about what might have been.

A bit more background: The first major league team I

rooted for was the Atlanta Braves. When they started losing in 2015, I shifted to my dad's Houston Astros. During 2020, I shifted again, this time away from being a fan of any one specific team. I started developing an interest and appreciation for all thirty teams and their histories.

For most of the twentieth century, caps worn by the players and umpires on the field had leather sweatbands instead of today's cotton. This intrigued me when I first learned about it. I set out to acquire an official MLB umpire cap with that leather band. After much searching, I acquired two from two sources, including current MLB umpire Joe West. It was after that that I started considering going to an umpire school. My logic was that if I ever became an umpire, I could have as many caps as I wanted. Attending umpire school had just been a fleeting thought in my mind for a few years going back to high school. I had never really considered it until mid-November 2020. I told my friends and family about my plan, and they all had my back, so I enrolled in the Wendelstedt Umpire School for 2021. My experience there is what my blog documented.

As I wrote this introduction in November 2020 - with my two umpire caps near at hand - I sensed a shift in my baseball life. I had put on baseball uniforms to play in Dixie Boys games, high school games, and Alternative Baseball Organization games, a league for people with autism and other special needs (I have Asperger's Syndrome, which is high on the Autism Spectrum), which is why I could play with them. But, other than ABO, I would soon be taking off that uniform for good and replacing it with a different kind of baseball uniform. Instead of a team logo on the front and a number on the back, my new uniform would have a league logo stitched onto the front and a number on the sleeve. It's interesting to consider how both uniforms represent organizations that are so similar, and yet so different at the same time. Maybe that's a bit too deep. It's still baseball, whether it's major leaguers playing their trade on the diamond, kids running around the backyard getting dirty and sweaty, or umpires working hard on the base paths. It's all part of the game. And yet, as important to the game as umpires are, it seems most people can't name a single Major League umpire. This species called Homo sapiens is a fascinating bunch (Or rather, a fascinating eight billion).

I may have been long-winded to introduce myself, and I hope I didn't bore you. I just figured that I should provide background information so you might feel closer to the journey I'm about to take you on. I humbly thank you once again for acquiring my book, and I sincerely hope you will enjoy this collection of tales as much as I enjoyed retelling them. God bless...

December 31, 2020

It's almost time for me to put my words into action and head down to Ormond Beach, FL, to learn as much as possible about baseball and umpiring. That will happen tomorrow, the same day the calendar turns to a new year, which I'm sure many people look forward to. I don't really care too much because it's just the calendar turning another day, month, year, hour, minute, second, and AM... well ok, it is kind of cool, but I need to get some sleep tonight, so I'll be ready to go tomorrow. I'll get up around seven, shower, prepare for the day, and finish packing the car. I think a friend or two will stop by before I leave, and I'll be on the road before I know it. How do I feel? I am anxious because I've never done anything like this before, and I want everything to go smoothly (And I don't want to forget anything). Still, I know I'm going somewhere where I'll likely fit right in and have a lot of fun learning about stuff I am genuinely interested in. Shoot, I get to sit in a classroom and be taught every word in the official baseball rulebook - my kind of class. If I forget anything, it will likely be something I can get somehow while I'm down there. This is one of those times I wish I could snap my fingers and be there. That would eliminate packing belongings into the car, paying for gasoline, and the overall hassle of travel. I wonder how many trips people would go on if that were possible.

January 1, 2021

I'm writing this in a hotel room more than 300 miles away from home. The school has us staying here at the Best Western Castillo Del Sol hotel (Which I'm not too impressed with so far. It is more like a multi-story motel with a smell that's the combination of cigarettes and dingy). I'll do some more unpacking and settle in when my roommate gets here tomorrow. I'm not sure who it will be, but I hope it's someone who's cooperative and fun, not annoying. Though people who know me may say I'm annoying, I should be used to it. This should be interesting. I'll be here for a month, going back and forth between here and some baseball fields I think I passed on my way into town. Other than other students and instructors, there are no family or friends. Strange, but I guess that's how life goes. You grow older with others to get away from others. The drive down wasn't too bad. No one came by before I left, so my family was there to send me off. When I left, it was raining back in Phenix City, so I had to deal with that until I reached Sylvester, GA. According to Google Maps, there were a lot of speed traps on my way down, but luckily, there was a pickup towing what I guess is a towable RV in front of me, so I just stayed behind it because it wasn't going too fast. I think there are some telltale signs (Not necessarily literal) that you're in a certain state that you can notice when driving. In Alabama, it's Alexander Shunnarah (who is an attorney) and his billboards. In Georgia, at least for right now, there are senate runoff election signs of all sorts. And in Florida, palm trees. Other than a gas station stop that may not have even been necessary, I didn't make any stops coming down here. I wanted to get here and get settled as soon as possible. Tomorrow morning is registration, and I don't have to check out of this room because the instructors are going to keep me in this same room (305, in case you ever go to that hotel and want to touch the same doorknob I did) so I'll just get showered and go down there to get everything done. Meeting other students, instructors, and MLB umpires should be fun and I'm looking forward to it. So how am I feeling, you ask? Physically, I'll just get some rest tonight, but the mental aspect of being this far away was pretty unsettling. I'm sure I'll be fine as the days go by, but until then, I guess I need to find something to eat and watch on TV. And even that may not be enough.

January 2

The first day of the Wendelstedt Umpire School was today, and I'm starting to relax a little more now that some things are starting up. This morning was registration, so I woke up at seven. When I got up, I decided to take my time getting showered and dressed because I figured that if I went down there too soon, they would give me a roommate quickly. But if I took my time and waited, they may have everyone assigned to each room at that point, and there won't be anyone left to put in my room. I'm writing this at 11:20 this morning, so I still don't know if that worked, but registration lasts a good portion of the day today, so I'll see what happens. After putting on my light blue dress shirt, navy sports coat, khaki pants, brown belt, socks, and shoes, I went down to the lobby, where a short line had already formed. It wasn't long before students were being called into the meeting room. When my turn came up, after I spoke with some other guys about where they had come from (And pointed out that where a large water hose was on the wall, the case said "fire hose." But shouldn't it say "water hose?" Certainly, fire doesn't shoot out of that hose otherwise, the hose would burn, and there wouldn't be a hose there on the wall to begin with because it would have burned). I went into the room, was greeted by some of the instructors, and had my glorious picture taken (What a lucky day for these guys, huh). Then I was told by Junior Valentine, the head classroom instructor, about a meeting later tonight, and they said they would text me about when to come down. To his left and right were MLB umpires. I could tell because they were wearing their MLB uniforms. The one to his left (possibly Jerry Lane) mentioned trying to have masks on whenever possible (I guess he would, considering he had on a cloth mask and a shield, because some people do that for some odd reason). I forked over my last five dollars and bought an official MLB mask, the same as the MLB umpires wore. I spent money on a tool used to enact socialism! Yeah, I'm sick, and not just because of the pizza I had last night. If anything else, it's a baseball memento to add to my collection of baseball stuff. He also said they don't know how good I'll be after this course, but that I will be better than when I came in. Learning more baseball stuff was fine by me. Behind those three men was another MLB umpire pacing the floor slowly. He was Hunter Wendelstedt, whose shirt had a World Series patch on the sleeve. There was also a chair right where they told me to stand for the picture and listen to the instructor, where there was a small duffle bag with the school logo on it, and all the apparel was inside. I unveiled the contents of the bag when I returned to my room. There was a blank black adjustable cap, four black school t-shirts, a black umpire uniform shirt, a pair of umpire pants, a 1/4 zip-up pullover (often called a "shell"), and a course manual with the Official Rules in it. Flipping through the book, I noticed a few pages at the back featuring pictures of baseball fields, presumably to illustrate where we go when the ball is hit or thrown in different places. However, the dugouts bothered me because the third base dugout said "HOME," and the first base dugout said "VISITOR."

Nooo, it should be the other way around. The home team should be on the first base side so that when a player scores, they have the convenience of simply jogging straight to the dugout without having to change direction much, and the visitors must touch the plate, then turn around to face their dugout, then jog to it. Little details make a big difference. How so? There was an instance during Mickey Mantle's career in which he had been so hung over from the night prior, that after he hit a home run in Yankee Stadium (The true original one, by the way) and got back to the first step of the home dugout on the first base side, he threw up right then and there. Maybe he would've done it in front of all the fans if he had more time to turn around and jog back to the dugout. You don't want the kids to see that.

My roommate, Xavier Wood, did eventually show up. Coincidentally, my best friend's name is also Xavier (Dye). It has been entirely too long since I last saw him. Anyway, my roommate told me he wouldn't be a slob, and he seemed nice. However, he curses more than I'd like and has a vape, but there is no cause for me to keep complaining when I have a job to do.

But he is also part of the crew I'll be with for the course. The crews have six people and are named after Hall of Fame umpires. My team name was Donatelli. So we went up to the school campus for our first meeting and did a role call where we said our name, where we came from, and whether we had a roommate. After that, the classroom instructor discussed how we should approach everything. He stated that we should not be afraid to ask questions and make mistakes now so we could move on to the next one. He is definitely okay with mistakes as he has had some experience with seeing them, and because of them, there have apparently been rule changes because of things that happened at the school. We signed a waiver and a cancellation agreement just in case we have to cancel enrollment for some reason. MLB umpire Jansen Visconti taught us how to put on our cap and mask correctly. Then Hunter Wendelstedt said that because the class is smaller this year, there was a little more flexibility with lesson plans. This school is still subject to the same rules as other Florida schools, and they might bring back some older lessons from when the school was named after other people. So, in the end, when we had our final questions, I asked if there would be potential to learn how to use the outside chest protector, otherwise known as the "balloon." Wendelstedt said that he couldn't guarantee it but that Jerry Lane would probably know since he was one of the last to learn how to use that. But he said he might know someone even better: Cowboy Joe West. As I mentioned in a previous post, he is the one I had emailed and gotten an MLB umpire cap from, so to meet him, make that connection that I'm the one who was on the other end, and learn how to use the balloon from him was very exciting.

Tomorrow is Sunday, which is always an off day. Wendelstedt said they tried having class on a Sunday once, and God made it rain for all but two days for the remainder of the course, so they chose never to do that again, which is nice. In addition to getting my new umpire pants hemmed by the seamstress they'll bring in tomorrow, I'll practice that cap and mask, like they said. Yeah, I think I'm going to be fine.

January 3

While practicing the cap and mask techniques, I found that it's not as hard as I thought because I had already been doing it correctly, except my hands were switched. With the cap, the right hand is on the back, and the left hand is on the brim; the back goes on first, then the front. With the mask, the right hand is on the harness, and the left is on the lower left portion of the mask. Once again, it is back then front, going out then down to get the mask around the cap's brim. If we were taking the mask off, we would use the exact hand placement, reverse steps: out, then up. They said stuff would be implemented tomorrow, so I think I should be good.

The seamstress was also here to hem our new umpire pants. She was friendly and got us out of there pretty quickly. The raised plastic base was made of plastic with strips going in different directions, so it was rough to stand on, but it was only for a few seconds. There was also another lady there selling merchandise with the school logo. I passed today, but she said she would also be at the fields if I wanted to purchase something.

My roommate seems to be a social guy who often goes to other people's rooms, while I prefer to stay in. That's just what I'd prefer to do. It gives me time to read scriptures and write.

Tomorrow will be the first full day of learning. Classroom instruction is at nine, lunch, I presume, at noon, then fields, I guess, until they cover everything they need for that day. That's probably how each day will go except for the occasional Saturday when we'll skip classroom instruction and have the occasional class again at night after we get off the fields. I guess I'll see how often that happens.

Although this is an umpire school, a few of us have played before, including myself, and I'm sure those of us who have played still like to. We were asked to bring a fielding glove if we had one, so a few of us went out to throw on the beach, which is probably one of the only things that will get me on a beach. I'm sure we may draw a diamond in the sand at some point and practice calling some plays, especially considering that you can slide more easily in the sand. So I'll go out for that too. In fact, I'll probably do the sliding because it's fun to get dirt (or, in this case, sand) all in your pants, socks, and underwear as long as you're safe, especially if you do one of those slick swim slides to evade a tag. I almost pulled one off during a summer game at Troy University a couple of summers ago, but I got out at third trying to advance on a passed ball. The ball didn't go far away from the catcher, but it was still a close play.

I hope Jerry Layne was right yesterday at registration when he said we're here to have fun because that's how I will approach every day. They shouldn't make this course sound fun if they don't want fun. And heck, if they send me home because I'm having fun, I'll just remember a George Carlin quote: "If it requires a uniform, it's a worthless endeavor." I think you may agree with that, at least a little bit. Obviously, I know not to mess around or act a fool; I'm just talking about being in a state of fun while on the field. If they say I need to be super serious, this job isn't for me. I feel like I'm too... "different" to simply do something for a living that lots of other people do, too. I've thought about trying stand-up comedy, but I don't know if I'm THAT funny. I'm glad I live in this day and age where you can get paid for almost anything. Heck, porn actors have gotten paid for years. You see people all the time now working from home at these jobs that I don't even know what they are, but somehow, they get money. I probably wouldn't want to do that because I would still want to go places, but a fun job would be good (I guess that's everyone's fantasy, though. Oh well).

Anyway, I'm sure I'll have some fun down here and learn a lot. Considering my knowledge and interest in the game, I think I'd be a great umpire after this course. So many people believe this is a perfect fit. We'll see. I don't want to think too big and take myself too seriously right now. These next few weeks should be a great experience, so I want to soak it all in.

January 4

Today was the day that started what we all came down here for: umpire instruction. After getting up, showering, and waiting for my roommate to do the same, I drove to the campus where the classroom and fields were. Speaking of which, I need to tell Xavier not to use his smoking device in my car. Most of you would call it a vape, but as far as I'm concerned, it's close enough to smoking to where that's what it is. And smoking is drugs. Therefore, vape = drugs. I don't want that to damage or leave a scent in my VW. I can tell this guy is somewhat of a junkie, but if I keep my head down (except when tracking a pitch), I should be fine.

We started in the classroom at nine sharp—roll call, then some of the official rules. First, we used 1.01 and some of the ones that followed, and then we jumped around to things that applied to what the previous rule discussed. For example, 1.01 specified that baseball is a game played by two teams of nine players each on an enclosed field, with each team under the direction of a manager and officiated by one or more umpires (those aren't the exact words). From there, we discussed other rules that pertained to the manager being appointed to the umpire-in-chief before the game (though today, that usually doesn't have to happen because managers are named before a season and are paid well). If the manager leaves the game, such as in an ejection, the team must designate the substitute, or the umpire-in-chief will do it for them.

Then Junior, our instructor, told us a story from when he was calling a game in the low minors. He ejected the manager and then went over to their dugout to find out who the next manager would be. He asked the old pitching coach if it would be him because he looked like he was taking over, but the coach didn't respond. Junior asked again, and he still without a response. So, like the funny guy he seems to be, he went over to the backup catcher and told him that he was the acting manager. Then the pitching coach argued, saying he was the manager, but Junior said no—he had his chance—so the backup catcher ran the rest of the game. If I ever have that kind of opportunity, I'm naming the injured relief pitcher in the bullpen the manager because that's my kind of move.

Other than that, we covered simple stuff, like the objectives of the offense and defense, nine defensive players, and eight of them in fair territory (anywhere in fair territory, by the way. The shortstop can play on the right field warning track if he so desires). But a new rule states that whoever is closest to first base must wear the first base mitt. Suppose the first baseman plays in a bunt situation, and the second baseman moves closer to the first base to prepare for a play. In that case, if the second baseman is closer to first base than the first baseman, the second baseman must wear the first baseman's mitt. That is interesting stuff, and I will totally be referring to it next time I see it happen on TV.

Two base coaches per team, both in their respective coach's box, must wear helmets after a coach died from being hit a long time ago. They must remain in the coach's box until the ball passes them, and there should be no touching players unless exchanging equipment (those two are usually not enforced too much to ensure some level of decency).

Then, some stuff about calling "Time" and "Play" (not "Play Ball," presumably to keep in fashion with one-word commands), dealing with light conditions, and some definitions of strike zone, foul tip, strike, and ball.

Then we got to the fields. The luscious green and orange were refreshing to see again, and it was great to be on a field because I don't get that opportunity much anymore (unless I go walk around Golden Park because the gates are open during the week). The field was neatly chalked, and the foul poles and the line on the outfield wall were a pure yellow.

In the outfield, we did formations. We stood in columns with our crews to make a grid over the outfield grass in left field, then went through "safe," "out," "strike," and "ball" calls, calling "time" after three strikes and four balls. Those are way more detailed than you think, so it was right up my alley. Watching some instructors show us stuff on the field around home plate was great. Seeing baseball stuff on an immaculate surface like a ballfield is very satisfying, at least to me.

Soon, it was lunchtime. We place what we want every night on Google Classroom, something I forgot to mention last night. I ordered a chicken sandwich because I wanted to stay light on the first day, but it had a weird texture in my mouth. I expected more of a breaded chicken like at Chick-Fil-A or Popeyes, not grilled chicken. So I'll get something else for tomorrow.

After lunch and more formations, which got boring after a while, we had another demonstration where they showed us to stand on one of the foul lines (whichever team just hit, go to the opposite side), tell the pitcher our name, "plate umpire," then "one more pitch." After the last warmup pitch, we brush the plate, stand back, and be sure of the five things that must be there to start the game (nine defensive players, eight of which in fair territory, with the catcher being the exception, two base coaches, pitcher on the rubber with the ball, catcher in the catcher's box, and a batter in the batter's box), put our mask on, then go behind the plate and put the ball in play (point forward and yell "play") when the pitcher is on the rubber. Then we get into the slot position we were taught earlier (between the batter and catcher, the closest foot is always the one closest to the slot. For example, a right-handed batter, left slot foot), use the proper mechanics we were also taught earlier to track the pitch, and make a call. We did this down the left field line with our crews, so every crew had their own space to do this stuff and an instructor to guide us. Reed Basner was over the crew I'm in. I got better as I went along like most of us probably did. After all of that, we got into formation one more time and did everything once more. When we were about to start, Junior told some kind of joke. I don't remember what it was, but he didn't hear any laughing, so he said, "Y'all must not think I'm funny." Since he was near me when he said it, I said that we were laughing but that he couldn't see our mouths moving because of the face coverings. He then called my bluff, saying he could still hear laughter but didn't. I guess if I don't remember what the joke was, it wasn't too impressive. I don't think it was that bad, but oh well— he'll have plenty more chances. After the last formation, we were released. I started writing this not too long after I got back to the hotel room.

No one here knows I'm writing this, nor does anyone else have access to it, and I plan to keep both of those statements true. Although, with my sort of nosy roommate, I'll see how long I can do this while he's in the room. The good thing is he isn't here right now, and he goes to hang out with some other guys pretty often, so that gives me time to write these things and do other stuff alone. I'm thinking about going to Dunkin' Donuts across the street for dinner. I can't say I've tried that before.

January 5

Day two, and a lot of progress has already been made. I woke up this morning, got ready, and went to get breakfast, which is part of the meal plan. This morning, eggs and bacon were mixed together, and yogurt was mixed with fruit. I prefer smooth yogurt, so I didn't eat it.

In class today, we started with the basics of the two-man umpire system, then covered field and equipment dimensions from the rulebook and the uniform rules. One of my biggest gripes in baseball is Rule 3.03 (a), which states that all players must wear uniforms identical in color, trim, and style, and (c), which states that no player whose uniform doesn't conform to that of his teammates shall be permitted to participate in a game. What about the ongoing baseball fashion debate of knicker-length pants and visible socks vs. full-length trousers? Different players on every team use both styles, yet the leagues give no fines. So, which is it? Do the players need to wear identical uniforms or not?

We went over how the pitcher cannot use white or grey gloves or sleeves, equipment specifications, and then a story: Junior told us about a game when a manager complained to the home plate umpire (not Junior) about the batter's bat having too much pine tar. The plate umpire looked at it, then, instead of giving it back to the batter and telling him to get a different one, he threw it to the dugout, yelling, "Too much pine tar!" The batter sheepishly got another one, but the umpire inspected it and threw it to the dugout, yelling again, "Too much pine tar!" The batter got another one and asked if that bat had too much pine tar on it, after which the umpire ejected him.

One of the equipment and uniform specifications mentioned in the rules is that "undue commercialization" is not allowed. Good, keep it that way. Don't be like the NBA, which has sold itself and its teams out to the corporate swine of our crumbling society. Although Junior said he thinks that will end soon, I sort of wanted to slap him paler than he admitted he was earlier when mentioning a demonstration, they usually do when discussing the PANTONE 14 color spectrum that the rules say are allowed on gloves (in which all the instructors stand up there from darkest to palest). But I didn't because he was already frustrated that we weren't laughing at all his jokes. When we said the masks were the problem, he asked if anyone would feel uncomfortable if he took it off, which was met with a resounding no, so he took it off, and we all clapped. Garrett Forsythe then said the masks also make it harder for us to laugh, after which Junior said we're not taking ours off. Oh well.

When I get the discount code for the Gerry Davis Sports website, I may order a patent leather belt because they're cool. Those essentially replaced neckties a long time ago.

On the fields, we built off yesterday's plate stances and routines by adding passed ball drop steps followed by "Ball's in play" calls, the same drop steps used for catcher pop-ups followed by either "That's a catch" or "No catch," and where to run on a ground ball and base hit. Now, I feel like I'm becoming a better umpire.

Before the base hit and ground ball stuff, we had lunch. Today, I got the special for Tuesdays: country fried steak with mashed potatoes and corn. It was good, and I didn't feel bloated afterward. A great balance if you can find it. While eating, I noticed a baseball on top of a pole in the middle of the fields. This pole supported the netting that extended to other poles around the backstops, preventing balls from flying into the crowd. Interesting, but now there's no way to shut up the annoying mom (with a foul ball) who thinks if her son doesn't get a base hit, he won't make it to the big leagues and will have a pitiful life like she did.

After the last drill, we met at the podium behind field 3, where Jansen Visconti (MLB umpire), Junior, and Hunter Wendelstedt (MLB umpire and owner of the school). He told us good work and to keep working on drop steps because they're vital to everything umpires do. Hunter said he saw a lot of good stuff, so he called off formation to end with, and we were released. It didn't really matter to me, but I'm hoping that with the progress we're making, we can get ahead of schedule with lesson plans and have more time to learn some of that other stuff from previous eras of the umpire school, as Hunter said on the introductory day, as well as have a little more downtime. I took one more look at Hunter's green MLB St. Patrick's Day cap, then got my stuff and went on my way. Xavier rode with someone else who took him to a bank to get a cashier's check, so I drove back to the hotel, changed clothes, and walked back to Dunkin' Donuts. He came in soon after, and while I've been writing this, some other guys have been coming in and out, but I think that's over now.

I'm hoping there will be opportunities to show my baseball knowledge and expertise and impress everyone because I know all sorts of baseball stuff (not just umpire stuff) off the top of my head. Today, when discussing field dimensions and how fields built after 1958 must be a certain size, Junior wondered what current ballpark was the last to be built before then. Of course, I knew the answer: Fenway Park. But he thought it was Dodger Stadium, so he asked us to Google when the Dodgers moved to LA. I knew that question was irrelevant because Dodger Stadium wasn't built (or at least didn't open) until 1962, so it didn't fit into the pre-1958 flexibility. And yes, I also knew when the Dodgers moved to LA—1958, coincidentally the same year the Giants did. The Dodgers played in LA Memorial Coliseum until '62, and the Giants played at Seals Stadium (named after the Pacific Coast League (a minor league) team that played there, the San Francisco Seals) until 1960 when Candlestick Park opened. Candlestick Park and today's Oakland Coliseum looked great as baseball-only parks before football moved in (yet another thing football has ruined for America), and the outfield was fitted with tons more seats. Go look up pictures of Candlestick and the O.co from their first seasons, and you'll see what I'm talking about.

Unfortunately, I didn't speak up about any of that in the class for some reason. Obviously, a lot of that wasn't relevant today, but the parts that were would have made me look really educated, which might have impressed the instructors. I'm not trying to be arrogant, but I think that would be something they might consider when deciding on placing me in a league this summer—that I am knowledgeable, and I dare say "passionate," about the game. That might make them think that I would really appreciate the job, and everyone likes being able to do something for others that they know will be appreciated. I'm also smart about psychology.

Anyway, dinner is in less than an hour, so I'll head down there to get a box and bring it back up to my room at seven.

January 6

At the end of today's instruction, Hunter told us that today is the hardest day of umpire school. He may or may not be right.

In the classroom, after our first 10-question test (on which I got all but one question right), we covered when a batter becomes a runner, when a runner is out, a hit by pitch, batters being inside the batter's box, and what happens when they're not, tags, and dead balls. Something you may or may not know about me is that I tend to be a ball magnet when I'm playing baseball, meaning I get hit by pitches a lot. Because of this, sometimes I'll look for pitches close to me and stand completely still so I can get hit and go to first base to use my wheels. Apparently, that's not something you should mention at umpire school.

When discussing hit-by-pitch, I asked Junior if we could call the batter back if we thought they intentionally tried to get hit. I started the question by telling him that one time in a stickball game, a pitch was heading for my knees, so I disguised a lean-in with my knees as a stride. It wasn't hard because your knees naturally go forward slightly in a stride, so it wasn't entirely a trick move. While I was explaining this, Junior interrupted, saying, "Oh, so you're a cheater?" I tried to explain further, but that only reassured him that I had cheated. Eventually, he answered my question, but afterward, he said he would keep a close eye on me during drills today to ensure I was not cheating. He then asked if I wanted to apologize to baseball for cheating. I thought, whatever, I'll do it. So I did, and I got an answer somewhere buried in that debacle. Mind you, when we ask a question, we're supposed to stand up, say our name, and then ask, so I stood the whole time.

Looking back, Hunter may have been right. At the field, we incorporated fair/foul calls and mechanics into formation and drills and more base hit and fly ball scenarios. I ordered a cheeseburger for lunch because the Google Classroom said the special for Wednesdays was a sloppy joe, which I didn't want, but the Google Form where we make our choice said meatloaf, which I did want. Since I didn't want to be uncertain of getting what I wanted, I ordered something regular.

At the end of the day, we met at the small stand again, where Jansen, Junior, and Hunter gave some closing remarks. They're really impressed with how we're picking up on everything, which is great because we can move along quicker. Jansen said that eventually, we will hit a brick wall (while Junior punched his fist into his upright hand to simulate that) because it happens to every class, but that when we do, we shouldn't get discouraged because we will come out better because of it. Junior said that tomorrow, we will have our second test, which will be on dimensions. Hunter called off formation for a consecutive day, which I figured was irregular, and it was because Jansen said it was unusual for Hunter to do that. Hunter also said that tomorrow is the fun day—plays at first, the day he said he finds out if he has job security. He also said that after instruction, he would order a bunch of pizzas and hang by the pool so we could get to know people and talk baseball and stuff.

After they released us, I got some more information on the Gerry Davis Sports promo code. I spoke to Hunter for a second when he asked if I was having fun, and I said yes because there's nothing like 60-degree weather in January. He added, "And on a baseball field," which makes perfect sense. After that, a guy in my crew named Jeff and I took a couple of minutes to sharpen up on some drop steps, then left. On the way back to the hotel, at the traffic light just before a bridge, we had to go over the corner of the street closest to me on my right, which was filled with Trump and other right-wing supporters. Interestingly enough, once the light turned green and I passed them, on the adjacent corner were some BLM and Antifa supporters. It has been an eventful day in the political realm, but I'm here to call people safe and out, not political words.

January 7

I went to get breakfast this morning, but no one was serving it. I guess they didn't have it today. So, I went hungry during class but had a cheeseburger for lunch because I was skeptical about the pork chops special for Thursdays. After seeing them today, though, I may get them next week.

In class, after two tests (when Junior was collecting the first one, he asked if I cheated on it, and I responded with a shake of the head), we covered more two-man system stuff, and then force plays and what they are, and aren't, as well as runners touching bases and the fun that can come with those. For example, if a runner tries to get out of the way of a tag, he's out because the runner's lane is only three feet wide—not very wide at all. Essentially, any attempt to avoid a tag would make the runner out. We also covered what happens if a base comes out of the ground (I've never seen that happen before during play) and what to do if two runners are on one base.

We covered and practiced base umpire stuff at the fields, like plays at first base and where to go on base hits to each part of the outfield. The last thing we did was a game where we called plays at first. You would think it would just be a matter of reading the runner's foot and hearing the pop of the mitt, but they mostly made the ball do crazy stuff, and we had to make extraneous calls like "off the bag," "on the ground," "on the tag," and other things. It was more complicated than you'd think. The losing team had to do formation, and the winning team led it. My team lost because there was too much complaining (not from me), so Jansen called it. After the closing announcements, we headed back to get ready for the little pool party at the hotel.

The pool party was nice. It was cold, but a lot of us went to the pool deck and just talked about stuff, mostly umpiring stories and the logistics of umpiring and coming up through the different levels. Jansen and Hunter were both there, with Jansen mainly talking with some of the guys and shooting the bull about umpire stuff. Hunter was kind of being a mentor to anyone who came up to him. While showing a plate stance to some students, his foot slipped, and he joked with Junior, saying he was going to be working this season because of an injury.

I talked to Hunter and told him I was having fun and learning a lot and that I already felt like I was better than when I came in. He said if I needed anything, I need to go to any of the instructors, him, or anyone else. I told him that I was the one who asked him about the balloon chest protector in the introductory meeting, and he said, "There's gonna be a special day," which, of course, sounds exciting. I recalled that he mentioned Joe West when I asked him, and he replied again with, "There's gonna be a special day," and I would enjoy it. He didn't say what day it would be, but that's probably the point.

I then went over to Jansen, who got called up to MLB full-time a year ago or so. He talked to a few guys in a circle and told a story about traveling with Joe West alone (just the two of them) out of O'Hare Airport in Chicago. When they arrived, West nudged him and said, "Watch this, kid" (Jansen illustrated the nudge by nudging me). Among West's large suitcases that he always has and must check in was a briefcase that got stopped by the metal detector. The security staff was going through it to find what was causing the issue, and they pulled out all of his World Series and All-Star Game rings. Apparently, he always brings those everywhere. Jansen told us that West eats up the attention and loves it when people recognize him (maybe that's why his email is easily accessible).

Some other things Jansen mentioned were about how the replay room works and that starting next season (because 2020 was shortened), umpires will have microphones so the fans can hear them. After replays, they will announce the call like football does now. Baseball is changing, as I can tell by the new pivot move that MLB is looking into because it's safer for umpires.

January 8

I've developed a routine, so today started like most other days. I woke up at 7, got ready for the day, and headed over for class. We discussed more two-man system stuff and appeals, with Junior keeping the "cheater" stabs coming.

On the field, we drilled pause-read-react situations on fly balls. They said this is probably the hardest thing in the two-man umpire system, and I see why. Having to decide what call to make, what mechanic goes with it, and then doing whatever comes next is a lot. It's possible, but takes practice, which is why we're here.

After we were done, during closing remarks, Junior told us a joke about some pirates (actual pirates, not the ones in Pittsburgh, as it turns out). I think it went something like this, with the explicit words replaced with cleaner ones:

"Two older pirates would always sit at a bar for a while, and one day, one of them said that he wanted to go fight in a war. The other asked why because they already had a great life obtaining treasures. The first pirate said he thought this might be his last opportunity to do something like this, so he wanted to do it. The other one said he wasn't going but would be sitting right in that

chair when he got back in a year. Sure enough, a year later, the pirate returns, and his friend is sitting in that chair. The friend notices the peg leg, hook hand, and eyepatch that the first pirate now has, and in response, he asks what happened. He said that a bomb took out his leg, a sword took out his hand, and some bird poop took out his eye. The other pirate said, "You don't lose your eye because of bird poop." The first one responded, "You do when it's your first day with your hook hand."

January 9

The first week of umpire school is now in my past. Not a bad week at all—in the span of eight days, I have traveled six hours by myself to an unfamiliar place, ordered two pizzas via phone (and don't be surprised if that happens again tonight), finished registration for the Wendelstedt Umpire School, started the school, learned how to put on a hat and a mask correctly, and...well, you've been reading, you know what all I've learned up to now. Pretty impressive for a pitiful 20-year-old male with a 50-year-old mind and a 5-year-old feel for unfamiliar things (which means not at all) like me.

To round out the first week, we had a long classroom day consisting of two tests, more two-man instruction, umpire guidelines, the infield fly rule, and another cheater stab from Junior. Thomas Pruitt, who is also in the Donatelli crew, wasn't there today because he's recovering from tearing his Achilles yesterday. He was the right fielder during my turn as the home plate umpire. When he was chasing after the ball, I guess he slipped or tripped on something in the outfield grass and got hurt. It turns out he tore his Achilles tendon.

We had a demonstration at the fields before our early lunch (because class was longer). I got the Saturday special—pulled pork with baked beans and coleslaw. I passed on the coleslaw, but everything else was good. After lunch and the pickoff and steal drills, there was another demonstration where they asked for eight guys who could play baseball and some runners. Of course, I can, so I tried to go to the dugout, but enough guys beat me. Oh well. We then did those drills over base hits, and the day was done after closing remarks. I stayed for a couple of minutes, threw in one of the bullpens, and then left.

Tomorrow we are off, and Xavier will be gone camping until the afternoon—plenty of time for me to write without raising any suspicion.

January 10

I think these off days are going to be very valuable. If we want to practice anything, we can go to the fields we use for umpire drills. They said they have bats and balls for use. I don't know if I'll take advantage of that, but it's good to know it's available. I've also been doing 100 squats, push-ups, and sit-ups every evening, which counts as a workout. Even if I got a gym membership here for the month, I would probably be too tired after instruction to want to go anyway, so there's no sense wasting the money.

I'm writing this at 5:30 today, and my roommate isn't back from camping yet. It's peaceful here by myself.

So far, we've gone over some of the basic stuff, and I'm sure there will be a little more, but we ought to be getting to some interesting material soon. It also seems like we've been going quickly with content, so hopefully, that will give us more time later in the course to have more downtime or to learn some of that other stuff from older eras of the school. I doubt it, but time will tell.

I think I'm doing well. I'm still learning because I've never umpired a game before, but I don't think I'm doing poorly. I hope I'll catch on more as the course goes on and I can get an opportunity to call some games this spring and summer. It'd be cool to get a cap and shirt from a league, if nothing else. As far as MLB aspirations go, that can't start this year because there aren't any MiLB jobs available, so I'd have to come back again next January to get a shot. Will I? That's a long way from now, and a lot can happen between now and the end of this course and between now and this time next year.

I found out that, as of right now, after I get done here, my family has scheduled a trip to Universal Orlando Resort, somewhere we've been to twice before and been pleasantly surprised. During a break at the fields, I checked my emails and saw a confirmation for the vacation. I began to speculate what that might be, so I asked my mother if that email had accidentally been sent to me. She sheepishly said yes. Surprise spoiled. But as of right now, at least I can look forward to that.

So I will have spent a little less than the first month and a half of 2021 at a Florida hotel room, first here, then in Orlando. So once I finally get back to Phenix City, don't nobody talk to me for about three days, because I'll be asleep. After that, though, I can call a ballgame if anyone needs me to.

Being away from home, it's hard to eat right. My stomach is probably getting tired of pizza and Coke. It's probably practice for being on the road as an umpire. Hey, as far as I'm concerned, a pro baseball career is a pro baseball career, whether it's playing, umpiring, managing, coaching, or anything else.

It's cold outside. I'm wearing my black umpire shirt. I haven't left the hotel room all day, and a few minutes ago, I looked over toward the door and expected to see a hallway leading towards a living room, like back home. But there wasn't one. I think I'm getting institutionalized, or I will be soon.

January 11

It's the first day of week two, and with the progress I feel like I'm making, I may become a pretty good umpire. I got the hang of some more things at the fields, but not before taking three tests (runs scoring, appeals, umpire guidelines), learning about awarding bases, and hearing two more cheater references in the classroom. Junior was talking about what players used to do—put the ball in their back pocket to fool runners when they got it back from the outfield on hits. He said he thinks Jose Altuve started it, and all the players thought it was cute, but it wasn't, and now there's a rule against it. After he said all that, someone else in the room said "Cheater." At first, I thought he was referring to me and I was confused, but then I figured out he was referring to Altuve. If this man was informed, he would know that Altuve didn't partake in that system, but as with a few of my friends, he probably thinks ignorance is bliss as it makes it easier for their tiny brains to sort out the world. However, there are easy explanations or solutions only for those who are uninformed. I'll just get a job out of here and have the right to shut up anyone I please.

We finally got a warm day at the fields today, so we had great weather to eat lunch (I got the lasagna special), watch demonstrations, and practice fly balls with runners on first and double play footwork. I made a lot of progress today and feel like I'm shaping into a better umpire. Although, as far as my player skills go, I was playing third base today for a drill, and one ball got under me, and the next one, I made a poor throw before someone switched with me. I need to keep working on those skills as well. After one of my turns in double play footwork, Junior called me over to him, put his hand on my shoulder, and reassured me that he was just kidding with me about the cheater stuff (He didn't say "kidding"). I said I knew and didn't want anything to get in the way of me potentially going forward with umpiring, and he responded with a reassuring no. So that's good.

It was warm enough for me to take my pullover jacket off for the first time today, and my patent leather belt should come in this week. I also put a crease in my umpire cap a few days ago. I'm still working with the back of it, but the front is shaping up nicely. If you go and look at pictures or videos of umpires, you'll often see the front crowns of their caps kind of raised or with a curved line between the front and top of the cap. That is the crease I'm talking about. Why do umpires do this? The way it looks is the only answer I've ever come up with.

I often have days where I really want to get back on the field and play, and I think today was one of them. As I've said before, maybe my Heaven will have a diamond in it. Maybe Heaven is slightly different for everyone—what if wherever you think you go, that's where you're likely to go? Maybe Robin Williams is Ms. Doubtfire up there. Maybe Muhammad Ali is in a ring, but a diamond ring as a play on words. Maybe Jeffery Dahmer is under...actually let's not do that one.

I'm contemplating Dunkin' Donuts again (I can burn calories easily, so no worries of me slowing down because of any unhealthful stuff, at least as long as I don't make it a lifestyle), and I think that's about it until tomorrow. Hopefully, I can find somewhere to wash some clothes soon because I heard the washers and dryers at the hotel have broken.

January 12

Today was another productive day at umpire school, filled with tests, learning, and some new developments. We had tests on awarding bases and the infield fly rule, and we learned about catcher interference and obstruction in the classroom. Junior made another cheater reference, but it wasn't directed at me or anyone else this time.

I always get a bunch of emails from Google Classroom with our test scores, but today, there was another one titled "Job Placement Inquiry." It asked if we would accept a position in Indy ball or summer college wood bat ball, as those are the only jobs available this year. I told my parents about it but didn't hear much from them, so I said yes because that's what I was going to do anyway.

Job placement is starting to come up a bit, with guys talking about it and even a Frontier League representative stopping by after we were done today. I guess things work similarly to how pros and colleges recruit athletes, but I'm hoping this recruiting doesn't involve as much drama and abuse as I've heard about in some sports recruitment.

I need to correct something I said last week. I mentioned that the pictures of blank baseball fields in the course book had the home and visitor dugouts mixed up. It turns out they are written backward. If you put it in front of a mirror, it is correct.

It was a cooler day at the fields today, but we still drilled plate and base umpire responsibilities with a runner on second and time plays. We also revisited a drill we did last week to ensure we still had some fundamentals down. I chose the special for lunch: country fried steak with mashed potatoes and corn—good stuff. I always get water because I'm not taking the chance of getting a soda and then not performing well after lunch.

I have a Rawlings facemask with black metal bars and black-tan padding, as do two other guys, so I need to keep an eye on it to avoid confusing theirs with mine. During one of my turns today, when I was behind the plate with my mask on, I saw the ball coming in and realized the catcher wouldn't catch it. A moment later, I knew it was going to hit me, which it did in my left forearm. I didn't move a muscle because we're supposed to stay still to track the ball. I only moved when Junior asked if I was okay, and I nodded. Then he hit the fungo, and I carried on with my turn. No one is soft here at umpire school.

The main thing that keeps me going down here is perspective. Even if I have a rough day (which hasn't even really happened yet), I'm still blessed to be here, in Florida, by the beach, without family hanging over me. I get to go to a classroom setting and learn about baseball, then go out onto a baseball field, run around, and do drills. At the same time, other people I know may be at work, school, or maybe just bored. So, I must have a lot going right if my biggest problem is a small burning on my forearm after being hit by a baseball pitch.

I wanted to get this post up earlier because we got out earlier, so dinner will be in two hours from now instead of the usual one. I have some leftover doughnuts, too, so after I publish this, I'm mainly going to sit back, watch some Impractical Jokers (mindless TV), eat, and give my mind a rest because that's what our instructors said to do since they know a lot is on our minds and we're always thinking about what we need to do in a drill if a ball goes a certain way.

January 13

Halfway through week two and three-quarters through the first half of umpire school, I'm feeling the intensity of this basic portion. We've covered a lot of information and techniques, and while I've made significant progress, tomorrow will be the true test of whether I'm ready to call a game.

I skipped breakfast again this morning, which I need to stop doing since I need the energy. My crew was at the front of the classroom today as we learned about collisions at home plate and pitching motions. Later, we had a balk demonstration at the fields. This was valuable information that I'm eager to apply.

At the fields, we drilled scenarios with runners on first and second before and after lunch. Lunch was meatloaf, macaroni and cheese, and peas and carrots. It was delicious and felt like it was fueling my muscles directly. Despite trying to work out and eat right for some time now, I haven't seen significant results, mainly due to inconsistency. I've been contemplating using a gym here, but the potential exhaustion from umpire training and the cost makes it impractical.

When I return home, I plan to get back into morning workouts and buy protein-rich foods at Publix. However, studies suggest that evening workouts might be more effective, and non-processed, healthier foods are often more expensive. Getting my grocery job back would solve the income issue but could also cut into my evenings and burn more calories, making it difficult to gain muscle. Balancing all this seems challenging.

Perhaps being here for a month will work in my favor. My job might be more flexible when I return, and my family might cook more for me after being away. I try to stay optimistic.

During today's drills, I played the role of a baserunner and managed to avoid a tag at third base, only to be reminded to make straightforward plays for the umpires' benefit. It was a fair point, but I had to try it at least once.

We had a demonstration on control games, where an instructor puts a ball into play, and we must react, get into proper positions, and make calls. This will be the real test of how good I'm becoming, and we'll find out tomorrow.

We were released for the day after the drills and the balk demonstration. On my way back to the hotel, I again noticed the political signage on the street corners. It seems they do this every Wednesday.

January 14

I woke up and made sure to get breakfast this morning, something I knew I needed to do more consistently. It was a solid meal of eggs, bacon, oatmeal, and a waffle, which was perfect for fueling an active day ahead.

In class, we took tests on catcher's interference and obstruction. Apparently, a lot of people didn't do very well. I scored my lowest so far on the catcher's interference test with a 6/10, and I believe I got a 7/10 on the obstruction test. All my other scores have been 9/10 or higher. After the tests, we covered the first half of offensive interference. There's a lot of material to go through, so it took up most of the class.

Toward the end of class, Junior introduced us to "Top Tens," where we could come up with jokes about him. He said he's given us plenty of material and would give us more if needed. He looked at me and added, "I've given you a lot of s—," which is somewhat true. I'm curious to see how this will play out.

Outside, we demonstrated and drilled the infield fly rule. Because the drill is straightforward, they mixed in some base hits and fly balls. I can confidently say that I know the infield fly rule very well. Without looking at any notes, I can explain that with runners on 1st and 2nd or 1st, 2nd, and 3rd, and less than two outs, if a high fair fly ball can, in the umpire's judgment, be caught by an infielder (or someone positioned close to the infield for this rule) with ordinary effort, the batter is automatically out.

During one of my turns today (after lunch, when I had a cheeseburger), I was the base umpire, and a high fair fly ball was hit. Despite turning around with the wrong foot and stumbling for a split second, I still called "Infield fly" when I saw ordinary effort. When the shortstop dropped the ball, I did exactly what we were told: I yelled, "He's out, he's out, he's still out!" while giving the out mechanic and stepping forward. It was a good rep, and when I told Tom Fornarola, a current Double-A umpire, that I used the wrong foot to turn around, he sarcastically said, "Oh shut up, get back there." That felt good, especially going into...Control Games. This is essentially 21 outs for umpires, where an instructor hits fungos to fielders, and the umpires must position themselves correctly and make calls. My crew didn't go today, which was a bit disappointing because a Northwoods League representative was there. However, I know we'll get our turn soon.

After that and formation, we were released. Tomorrow they are incorporating cage work, where we will go into batting cages and call pitches. We're really getting into the nitty-gritty now, and there's more to come as we still need to go over handling situations with managers, coaches, and players. Plus, there's that "special day" Hunter mentioned. The basic portion of the course is almost over, but the fun might just be beginning.

January 15

I said yesterday that we were starting to get into the nitty-gritty. I was right. Breakfast this morning included a waffle, sausage patty, eggs, and oatmeal. After that, we finished up the offensive interference unit in the classroom. I also learned some details about this year's banquet. It will be held in the classroom instead of at the fancy hotel they usually use. There won't be any formal dress code unless you count umpire attire as formal wear, which I do, especially now that I got my patent leather belt today, which I am wearing as I write this. The banquet will be on the evening of February 1st, and evaluations and any job placements will be on the morning of the 2nd, finishing by noon at the latest. Since I don't have to book a flight back, I'll either follow my family to Universal Orlando Resort's Cabana Bay Beach Resort or meet them there. They've asked families not to come, so it looks like we had mixed up the dates, thinking the banquet was on the 2nd and evaluations on the 3rd.

Today, I participated in my first control game, partnered with a cool and energetic guy named ArRee, who is staying in his RV instead of a hotel room—very smart. I did pretty well behind the plate, but I felt a bit off as the base umpire, probably because you always feel like you need to be moving somewhere. Most of the base umpire's work involves standing in one spot and turning your head. I'll get it, though. Jeff is really impressed with my progress, which is always nice to hear. After my control game, I did some baserunning for the other control games (they always have other crews doing the running and fielding).

I haven't seen Hunter in a while, and Jansen wasn't there today either. I heard they were at some MLB function, which makes sense. Jerry is probably there, too.

The last thing we did today was a cage demonstration, showing us how cage work will be done. It's like a player drill altered to suit umpires. Instead of standing in the batter's box to hit the balls, we call the pitches behind the catcher. Another fascinating way that umpires and players aren't that different. Perhaps one day, I'll write a book to share that insight with the world.

I hope I have my new belt on correctly. It has the most complicated belt buckle I've ever seen. The leather creates a lot of friction, making it harder to work with. If I can get it on, I'll probably wear it tomorrow (when we'll likely start cage work) to see how it looks and feels over an extended period of time. I don't have a chest protector and shin guards yet, but I will wait and see if I go further with umpiring before splurging on those. I might buy an outside chest protector I found on Amazon for $30 at some point, but I'm not in a hurry and may decide to save that money.

I'm looking forward to live innings when I can wear my polo uniform shirt and look all official while calling my first real game. After my control game today, I know I can improve, but I think it will all click at some point, and my instincts will take over. And hey—it ain't nothing till I call it, so those other teams have to wait for me to decide anyway. As long as I'm hustling and doing my best, I can probably get the benefit of the doubt. That's what Jansen told us.

January 16

Today, we finished up the first half of the umpire course, which I believe covers the basics. On Monday, we're moving on to situations that people want to hear about, like dealing with managers and players, warnings, ejections, etc. Junior asked us not to record that day's lecture. We're allowed to record other lectures (though I don't), but not the ones that deal with situations. It should be interesting.

I started the day with eggs, bacon, a waffle, and lemonade for breakfast, then headed to the classroom to learn about umpire interference. How embarrassing would it feel to call "time" and send runners back to their bases because I got in the way? The same person calling interference is the same one who caused it— I guess I'll know it when it happens to me, because Junior said it will happen to everyone.

After that, we watched a bunch of clips of plays with different kinds of interference and obstruction, which was nice. Junior also said that if we have any plays we want them to look at in class, we should send them to the school email. So, I raised my hand and innocently asked what that email address was, and...I didn't get a direct answer. I forget what he said, but Junior started messing with me again in a serious tone, so I just stood there perplexed. After he finished a sentence, I said, "I don't know what to do." Then he asked, "You don't know what to do?" I hadn't the slightest idea of what he meant. He then told me to sit down, but everyone else in the classroom was telling me to "hold my ground," so, despite my concern over what might happen if I did, I stayed standing. Then Junior said he was kidding, and everyone started clapping that I held my ground. Then he told me two different email addresses, so I have a video link drafted in my Gmail account.

Soon after I caught my breath from that nerve-wracking moment, we went over to the fields while it was windy and cool for a rundown demonstration and drills before lunch, when I had another one of those burgers. After lunch, I got into another control game and did okay.

A 14-year-old kid named Michael was there today with his parents for his birthday. He's into umpiring and has apparently been on the news before for something (I think he has some sort of special need, but you might be hard-pressed to figure that out). He had an MLB umpire cap given to him from Jansen, a John Tumpane uniform shirt (I could tell because it had 74 on the sleeve, which was Tumpane's number), and a yellow wristband with a ribbon and MLB logo on it that they wear for some cause in August, though I forgot who he said that was from. He also had a Father's Day umpire mask with black and light blue pads, which looked very cool. At one point, while some of us were waiting to take our turn behind the plate during a drill, he was talking about what kind of mask he would want to buy and that he's never purchased a mask—all his had been given to him. And I thought to myself, "Whaaaaaaaattt? Looking at prices on official's websites, this lucky guy." Michael evidently had fun today, and I suspect that you'll be able to find him here as soon as he is old enough.

Tomorrow is an off day. I'll have dinner and maybe hang out with some other guys tonight. I'm considering taking tomorrow completely off from baseball. No grass/dirt, no ball, no glove, no bat, no cap, no belt...well, actually, I'm too skinny not to use a belt, but I may just put baseball in the back seat tomorrow so I can be refreshed come Monday for the real nitty gritty— situations and cage work.

January 17

Having an off day really feels good. I wish it was two days, like a weekend, but I know we have a lot of stuff to cover, such as situations tomorrow, which should be a fun way to start the day.

Today, I took my time waking up and went to an open athletic field with a few other guys to throw frisbees. Believe it or not, that's a sport! Afterward, I returned to the hotel and did laundry across the street because the washers and dryers don't work right now. The lady at the front desk said someone was coming tomorrow morning to fix them, so I hope that will do the trick because I'd rather not go to that laundromat again.

Later, a bunch of us went onto the beach and played baseball with a plastic ball and bat. Sometimes, people incorrectly refer to it as Wiffle Ball, which is a different sport. After that, I was hungry, so I went to Wendy's and got a couple of burgers and fries. I think dinner is macaroni and cheese and more burgers. I won't be hungry after all that.

Yesterday, during a turn behind the plate in a drill, I got hit by a pitch for the second time this week. Matt Carlyon, a Double-A umpire who came down a week or so ago, threw the pitch. The catcher got out of the way because he felt like he couldn't catch it, leaving my right thumb and index finger in the way of this hurling ball of horsehide. But just like last time, I stood completely still and took it like a man as everyone else reacted and asked if I was okay. I nodded, then the ball was hit, and I took my rep. That felt good.

Starting tomorrow, we are going to have the cages in action, as well as control games. I hope to keep learning and getting the hang of the stuff in control games because knowing when and where to look and go when different kinds of balls are hit in different places is a lot to think about. Yesterday, when I was the base umpire, a ground ball was hit to the second baseman, and I went to shade the runner toward third, completely forgetting I needed to give a call for the play at first. You can imagine how I felt after that.

I sent in the link to the play I want them to review in class at some point and another one dealing with ejections. I don't know if they'll go over them, but it's worth a shot.

I've heard these last two weeks will be rough, but I wouldn't know, so I guess I'll see. I'm just hoping to have fun, reinforce some of the things I need to work on, and get to the banquet and evaluations so I can get home. It will feel good to be home again, if only for a night before we leave for Universal Orlando Resort the next day. Why am I driving back home instead of just staying in Florida and meeting my family there? That way, we only have to keep up with one car. I know I'll be exhausted by the time I get home from Orlando, but until then, I'm going to hang on for two more weeks. The first two didn't go by too slowly, so maybe that will also be the case for these next two.

January 18

Starting week three feels like being so close yet so far from the finish line. Today began with breakfast tacos, and then we headed to the classroom where Junior taught us how to handle situations, including warnings, ejections, and reports. We started on these crucial topics today and will likely delve deeper as the week progresses.

After the classroom session, we moved to the fields for drills, with lasagna in between. We had two demonstrations: the first was about enforcing balks, but I can't remember the other one. I did a lot of baserunning to help make plays for the umpires, but I still got some good work in myself.

Hunter was back today after being gone all last week. He said he was proud of our progress and clarified the dates for the banquet and evaluations. The banquet seems to be more like a cookout in umpire attire, which will be the day after evaluations. This setup might lead to some tension if evaluations don't go well for some, but we'll see how it plays out.

Reflecting on my progress, I've made many mistakes and significant strides. I think I'll finish with decent test scores, but I wouldn't be surprised if they say I'm not quite ready for the professional level yet. However, with two weeks left, there's still time for me to improve and possibly earn some experience this summer.

Lately, I've been hanging out with some guys in their rooms. They're a fun group, though some are into smoking weed. They've offered me beers and smokes, but I've politely declined. I enjoy their company when they're sober but keep some distance to avoid second-hand smoke and any negative perceptions from others.

I miss my dog, Mollie, a 14-year-old West Highland White Terrier who's been with our family since I was in kindergarten. She's aged quite a bit, but she's still hanging in there. I hope she will still be there when I get back home.

I miss many people, so I'm trying to spend time with the folks here—they're who I have right now, and they are good people. They're also helpful for brainstorming ideas for the roast session at the end of the course. Everyone expects me to roast Junior, but I'm finding it easier to come up with material for some of the other instructors.

All in all, it's a mix of excitement and anxiety as I head into the final stretch. I look forward to seeing how much more I can learn and improve these last two weeks.

January 19

Today was productive, and I did pretty well. If I keep picking up crumb after crumb of insight, I might be able to call real games at some point.

Before heading to the classroom, breakfast was the usual— eggs, bacon, oatmeal, waffles, and lemonade. There, I aced the offensive interference test (which many others didn't do well) and the ejection test. Junior taught us about the designated hitter rule, which, as with everything so far, is more complicated than you'd think. Junior also told a joke about a woman who went shoe shopping, but I don't remember the details.

We started with an interference demonstration at the fields before getting into control games. I didn't do too badly in the first control game, and the same goes for the second one after lunch, which was country-fried steak and corn. On the last play of the second game, Junior had both runners on first and second stealing. The ball was hit to the outfield, but a throw coming back in went out of play. When a thrown ball goes out of play, if it's not the first play by an infielder, the base award is two bases at the time of the throw. My partner and I awarded the runner from first base to go to third base and the runner from second to score. Junior then had the fielders appeal that the runner from first left early. Initially, I thought he didn't, but after Junior's prompting, I remembered that the runner was stealing, so he didn't properly tag up. They appealed again, and I called "out." Then Junior had them appeal the runner from second base, and I called him out too for an "advantageous fourth out," taking the run off the board. My partner signaled "No run" to the figurative press box.

Outside of that, I did a bunch of baserunning to help make plays and thought about when and what kind of equipment I needed to get. I need a new pair of base shoes to replace the ones I've had for five years. I have a mask that will do, but I don't have a chest protector or shin guards. I'd love a $30 balloon chest protector, but those aren't allowed at the professional level anymore. I can just go to the Epic Sports website and get some good stuff cheap. That's where I got my first pair of umpire pants a couple of months ago. I'd love to wear a suit and call games, but that doesn't happen anymore, either.

Before we left the classroom to walk to the fields, Junior told us that if they recommend us to a league, that league may have its own requirements, like being clean-shaven or having no long hair. Those aren't an issue for me, except when I try to let my facial hair grow out, but I usually shave it pretty soon after it gets noticeable. Facial hair can dry out your skin, which isn't comfortable, and my red facial hair clashes with my head hair. I guess I could've tried it out while working at Publix and had to wear a facial covering.

Tomorrow is the 20th, meaning there are ten days left here. It won't be long before I'm done and have more knowledge than I did before. I'll be home and looking for somewhere to call games if I don't already have somewhere lined up. I'll finally have time to relax and unwind, something I've been looking forward to since I got here but have been hard-pressed to find. I look forward to seeing how I perform when I leave here and seeing family and friends again. However, I've found some routine and structure down here for the first time in a while. These are vital parts of comfort and success, so I'm not trying to wish this time away either. I know there will come a time in the next couple of months when I wish I were back here instead of somewhere else, like being bossed around by a customer service team leader. Something tells me he wouldn't be able to handle Junior. Every day is an opportunity I appreciate having, and I know better than to waste it away.

January 20

Well, today was the day we all knew was coming. Many of us didn't know if we should be happy or sad about it, but it was a day we knew would change the coming days and weeks ahead.

I'm talking about, of course, the introduction of live innings. This is a more formal version of control games, where there is still a full defense and two umpires, but instead of an instructor pitching and another one hitting fungos, other students are pitching and batting, so it's more like a real game. The instructors sit up on the podium behind the backstop and evaluate. After the two umpires finish, they go to the instructors and get told that they suck and to go home or get feedback on what they saw. We didn't do those today, but we had the demonstration after my second time in the cages. My crew (Donatelli, if you remember) was in cage one after class and cage two during control games. So, I got a few different opportunities to work on my stance, head height, mechanics, timing, and how to put on a chest protector. Umpire chest protectors are different from catcher's ones. They remind me of what I think football shoulder pads are probably like. During my first session in the cages, I gave Ben Engstrand (an A-ball umpire who looks like he still hasn't hit puberty yet) my phone so he could film me (because that's how we're being evaluated this year). I'll be a pro back there in no time.

Breakfast was a little different today: still a waffle and eggs, but they included a biscuit and gravy too, which is always good. In the classroom, we took a test on the designated hitter and covered substitutions. I also saw that Jansen was back today, so it's nice to see him showing off his MLB attire around here again, just like Hunter does and did again today.

After meatloaf, peas and carrots, and mac and cheese for lunch, we had an obstruction demonstration that we didn't drill, but they said they would include in control games now. My crew went to Cage 2, and after we finished there, we had the live innings demo. They're called innings because there are different innings that different crews will work, so the scoreboard on field one will be on to signal those. It will be interesting to see if everyone can make those work smoothly. Maybe if I know I'll be calling live innings ahead of time, I'll wear my black umpire polo shirt. Maybe.

The last thing we did today was a third strike call contest at the end-of-day announcements. We broke into our crews and chose someone to represent us in the competition. Each of them took their turn calling third strikes in front of the podium, and then the instructors gathered and chose the winner. Matt, the guy we chose, didn't win, but one person will be able to challenge the previous day's winner every day. I guess we'll see if that's one person at all, or one person from each crew.

January 21

This morning was the standard breakfast of eggs, bacon, waffles, and lemonade, but not a standard test in the classroom on substitutions. Instead of ten questions, we were given a lineup card and ten substitutions we had to make on it. It was pretty easy to me. We had to mark out names and write new ones. I made a 10/10. We then covered game suspensions, postponements, and games that were called due to weather or other stuff. It was more than you would think, and it was even more challenging for me to absorb it all because my seasonal allergies came back up today, and it wasn't pretty. I actually have a small headache coming on while I'm writing this. I will try to make this quick because I'm also very hungry.

At the fields, I got into another control game. I'm doing better on the bases, but I need to keep what I have at the plate. After that was lunch, where the special was smothered-in-gravy pork chops with mashed potatoes and green beans. I'm not usually one to eat potatoes (And don't say "Well, you eat fries" like an antagonist), but I did today because I knew it would be filling.

I'll go ahead and take a moment to describe the extremes of the people who serve our lunch. So, the first guy is definitely past his prime age, but he also has a belly in the front and back. How that happens, and his legs stay skinny, I don't know. The next guy is younger and in better shape, and while I don't know yet what he's high on, he definitely appears to be on something. Now, the guy who serves our breakfast and dinner is cool. Maybe we think that because we see him more often and, there's more opportunity for him to engage with us. Nevertheless, all of them are appreciated by all of us.

After lunch my crew went to the cages for the second straight day, which I don't mind. Once that was done and the control games were finished, we started some live innings. I wanted to hit, but they needed a ballboy, so I stepped up like I always do when I'm needed somewhere. At the end of day announcements, the instructors stressed that the defenders needed to make plays for the umpires and that if they couldn't, it would make live innings hard to do, so they'd stop doing them. Let me know if you think I should take my skillset to the outfield to help.

Another thing that happened at the end of day announcements was the third strike contest again. Marv, who won yesterday, went last, and my crew nominated me. There were some good ones, including Garrett's, which consisted of him spinning and slapping his thighs. Mine started with me quickly raising my right arm three times and making bell noises, such as for a knockout in boxing, then a punch-out. Soon after me was the crowd favorite (for some reason), Dave Jamski. His move was just a big stomp and punch-out, and after everything was done, the instructors convened and declared him the winner. There's no way his call beats mine, Garrett's, or Marv's from yesterday, but I'll be back.

January 22

Tough days will happen every now and then, and today may have been one of those days. Don't worry—I'm alright, but I was just dealing with a couple of things.

Breakfast was good (just the standard stuff we've had on previous days), and I did alright on a test about called and suspended games. We covered batting out of turn in class, which wasn't so bad. We then went to the fields for a demonstration on handling situations, which I was looking forward to. However, before that could get started, I received a message from my mom telling me that Hank Aaron, the legendary Milwaukee/Atlanta Brave and Milwaukee Brewer who, is second on the all-time home run list and simply one of the greatest and most underrated players ever, had died. I usually find out about such news through a notification from MLB At Bat or Yahoo News, so it was interesting hearing it from my mom because she worded it almost like he was someone in our family, using a teary eye emoji.

I never saw Aaron play, but I've always known his significance to baseball and the Braves. He came up not too long after Robinson and Mays did, and like Robinson but unlike Mays, Aaron dealt with the Jim Crow/segregationist prejudice that was prevalent at the time (Mays was sheltered from this by the Giants). Even twenty years after Aaron debuted in MLB and nearly thirty years after Robinson broke the unwritten color barrier, Aaron still faced fierce opposition toward his chase to break Babe Ruth's (who I believe is the most overrated athlete ever) career home run record. Much to the opposing fans' chagrin, Aaron hit 755 career homers, 41 more than Ruth. Aaron's toughness, skill (not necessarily talent, because talent is natural while skill is developed), and presence have rung through the ages and will likely never stop.

Hopefully, the Krispy Kreme Doughnut shop in Columbus can find a new owner, but more importantly, I hope that now Aaron can finally be given the level of credit and recognition he so deserved during his playing days.

After the demo, we drilled situations because, apparently, you can do that. There were two benches set up on either side of the home plate circle, and there would be a plate and base umpire, and two instructors acted as managers (not coaches, as one unlucky plate umpire would soon be heavily reassured by Tommy, who was acting as a manager at the time). So how did I do? If you know me, you probably think I heard something he said and made a funny and witty remark, and it started from there. Unfortunately, that is not something I am permitted to do. Will I make that mistake someday? Probably. But not today. I was behind the plate, and I called a couple of pitches that were high and inside strikes (because they were), and Matt, the other acting manager, was chirping to me, "That was high." I replied, "I had it in the zone." By this point, I was looking at him, and he repeated himself, saying that it was up (we were taught not to say "high" because then a manager can say, "Well, I think you're high right now," which could potentially create a whole other issue). I said again that I had it in the zone because that's where I saw it. Evidently, it went back and forth like that for a couple of sentences, which I didn't mean to do. When I sensed that this was holding up the game, and he said, "I say it was up," I went ahead with the hammer, took my mask off, and said, "Well, I say you're gone," and made the ejection mechanic, something that they didn't really discuss. Matt then got up toward me and kept on...

> Me: "I had it in the zone. It's okay to disagree, but we're not gonna hold up the game for this."

> Matt: "I'm not holding up the game."

> Me: "You're holding it up right now—you're a step away from entering my office." (Because he was a step outside the dirt circle around home plate.)

Then Tommy called it off and said that I did good, but to try to nip the back and forth sooner. I didn't even realize I was doing it, so I'll be sure to look out for that next time. But this drill is definitely different from others. In others, you're simply trying to maneuver your body in different ways and to different places to get into good positions, whereas in this one, it's about your words and thinking. Even though you know someone will probably be screaming at you in a minute, it still gives you an unsettling feeling because you don't know exactly who will say or do what.

After that, I got into another control game. I've gotten better on the bases, but I sensed my progress behind the plate starting to drift away, which isn't good. While I've made progress, I'm still not up to par with others in the class, and we're 75% complete. They said at the end of day announcements that if we still felt lost or if our heads were still spinning, to fear not, as we still have another week. Hopefully, I can make some final strides tomorrow and walk out of here to work and officiate a game next week.

After that, and eating baked ziti (basically a pasta/lasagna mix) for lunch, I have cage work again, this time with a video. Before we could get started, back in the control games (two other guys and I were in the cages waiting on the instructor to get down there), someone had a seizure in one of the dugouts. Eventually, a fire truck arrived, and I guess everything was okay. I don't know who it was or how they're doing now, but I know it stopped the show for a good bit.

I did well in the cages again, and I have two more video clips to review. After that, more live innings, and I was the ball boy again. I'll hit at some point, but not today, as today was the second straight day of my allergy issues. I still have some draining, congestion, and throat issues. Luckily, I have some medicine with me, and Jeff Wallace, the guy I sit next to in class who is a 60-year-old retired Navy veteran but still a relaxed, happy guy, brought a box of tissues because he knew I was dealing with that yesterday.

This comes after yesterday when he got a bunch of tissues from the bathroom during a break in the classroom and brought them to me. He was very kind and thoughtful, which I guess is how he is. I heard him say that his son, who lives only an hour away from here, had an allergic reaction to something, so they had to take him to the hospital a few days ago. I guess it happened after we finished the day one evening because he never missed a day, was late or left early. I hope everything turned out well for him.

Once the innings were done, we had end-of-day announcements and the strike three call contest, and then we were done.

January 23

Today is done, and so is 3/4 of umpire school. With one week left, I likely am not up to par with where I should be, but I am better than when I came in, at least at two-man umpiring. We haven't even touched on three and four-man umpiring yet, and I'm starting to doubt if we will.

It was a standard breakfast of eggs and bacon, but French toast today was good and surprisingly easy to cut with a fork. In class, we took a test on batting out of turn and covered spectator interference, authorized personnel, and Junior made the executive decision to also cover forfeited games, which rounded out our classroom lectures. We will test them on Monday, and then we will be through with the classroom portion.

At the fields, I played two control games, one before and one after pulling pork and beans for lunch. In total, I had two turns as the base umpire and two as the plate umpire. On the bases, I was great, while on the plate, I was okay. In my second turn, I messed up a time play (not a "timing" play). After that, my crew got another turn in the cages (well, everyone in my crew except Frank, who had to get ready for a live inning). I've been doing well in the cages, except for some inconsistent timing between my strike and ball calls, which is an easy fix. Once we were done there, we joined in batting in the innings, and I took two at-bats, which I flew out. In my defense, I'm not here to swing but to call swinging strikes. And the same goes for the rest of us.

If this were a baseball player's school (which probably wouldn't be a bad idea—classroom sessions in the morning, then coaching in the afternoon), and we prepared ourselves to play and treated our bodies as such, then I'm sure we'd be better hitters, runners, and fielders. But once again, that's not what we paid up to $5K to come here for.

After innings, we had end-of-day announcements, the strike three contest where Mike MacStudy from my crew, who shaved his huge beard off yesterday and is almost unrecognizable now, won. Then, we were released for the weekend. Tomorrow is Sunday, which means a day off, so I don't intend to leave the hotel room for much except for breakfast and dinner because our guy still does those on-off days, which I didn't know until this week.

Only one more week until I return home and try to develop a routine for 2021, because I've been here for all of this year. Hopefully, I can get back to working out in the mornings and find some good food to eat to help me grow. I have some ideas on different things I can do, but I'll have to wait and see how long I can go without returning to a job. If I do, I will try to get a permanent schedule to keep whatever routine I develop for myself. I probably have slipped up on eating healthy this month (though I've tried to eat all my breakfasts, lunches, and dinners provided because those are cooked well and probably do help), but everyone does that when they're away from routine, and they have to get by with something.

But yeah, with umpire school and then the trip to Universal Studios, I'll have spent the first month and a week of 2021 in Florida. When all that is done, I'll probably take some time to sit down with my parents and see what all I want and need to do since I'll not only be back home, but I'll have a lot of free time because I'm not employed or enrolled in school after I graduate from this one. I'm sure I can figure something out. I haven't seen Xavier since I returned from the fields, so I need to look for him when I get dinner.

January 24

Today is our break before we start the home stretch of umpire school. I think we all needed it, and I had fun for the most part.

I woke up at seven as usual to get breakfast, but I later discovered that our guy serves breakfast at eight on Sundays, so I was too early. That sucked, but I went back to the room, got showered and ready for the day, then started doing some research and note-taking on the two-man umpire system because I'm still struggling with remembering everything to do, so I wanted to reinforce some things and drill them in more. I then invited some guys to go to either the beach or the fields to do some stuff, but no one came with me, so I went to the beach and, with my feet, drew up a complete baseball field with three bases, home plate, base, and foul lines, pitcher's mound and rubber, batter's, catcher's, and coach's boxes, on-deck circle, and dugout, and it looked great. The guys I invited, as well as a few other older guys, all came out to their balcony and were impressed. I took some pictures of it, partly because my mom wants me to take pictures while I'm down here. The cars drove by on the beach (because that's allowed here), and later in the day, the tide, decided that my field wouldn't last very long, but it was fun while it lasted.

Later, those guys went out there to throw, so I joined them, and while I was trying to restore the parts of my field that the tide had taken out, a guy named Kolton, who we call Pete because he looks like Pete Davidson, was kind enough to help me out with the first base line, which was closest to the water. As we were doing this, a wave came up and soaked my shoes, socks, and bottoms of my jeans. That was uncomfortable, so I changed into some shorts, and by that time, everyone had come inside, so I went to their room to hang out with them. Eventually, I returned to my room to put my other tennis shoes on since I had been walking barefoot because the other shoes were soaked.

This upcoming week will consist of a test tomorrow morning to round out the classroom, more control games, cage work, and live innings. Hunter talked about that special (evaluation) day, and the cookout will round out the course. It'll be interesting to see what we do later in the week. Still, until then, the instructors expect us to know our primary responsibilities, such as fair/foul, catch/no catch, and rotations, so that's what I was freshening up on today because I don't want to mess up on those.

Dinner will be in about ten minutes, and I want to take some of my notes to the room where we all hang out so they can help me. I think this is going to round out our last off day of the course, because next Sunday is supposed to be the cookout, and I'll likely leave for home either that day if everything gets done early enough or the day after on February 1st. I don't want to leave if many people, particularly the instructors, are still around, so I think I'll probably leave on the 1st. Although a few people may want me to stay until the second because we have the hotel until then, because we have all bonded, I also want to get home and see my family, especially my dog*, again, and do some things to prepare for Universal Studios. (*Most people, especially people from other parts of the country who are here at umpire school with me, would say that I say "dawg" instead of "dog." They would be right.)

January 25

Today, we had our final two tests: one on spectator interference, which I aced with a 10/10, and another on forfeited games, where I scored a 7/10. These tests concluded all our classroom work except for the top ten roast session, which will also be held in the classroom.

After the tests, we headed out to the fields for an ejection demonstration by the plate umpire, followed by formation, and then went straight into control games. I didn't do too badly, but I still need to reinforce some of my responsibilities as the plate umpire. I was hoping to do well while Hunter was watching. After that, the instructors noticed our double-play footwork was off, so we drilled that until lunch. For lunch, I just had a cheeseburger. My double-play footwork is pretty good, but I need to watch a few little things to ensure I get it right.

After lunch, we started live innings, but two crews, including mine, were sent to the cages. Mitch, a young instructor whose first year here was last year, worked with us on our strike three calls, which was definitely fun. He knows what kind of calls work with different body types because it does make a difference. For example, taller guys may only need one motion, while smaller-framed guys can get away with two motions. I'll keep experimenting to see what works for me, although I'm starting to lean toward the Hallion. You know how baseball players will fool around on the field, try to make great defensive plays at shortstop, and yell "Jeter" while they're doing it? Well, the umpire equivalent is the Hallion, created by Tom Hallion. Look it up. Derek Stevenson, one of my friends here, likes it and has mastered it. He gave me some pointers on it, so I might use it if I can get it right.

After cage work, I went to hit in the live innings and grounded out, only because I wasn't running full speed (since we're only trying to make plays for the umpires). Otherwise, I would've beaten it out. After a while, they started to go through all the umpires they had scheduled for innings and began calling more to get ready, including my roommate. Not too long after that, I put my helmet down to use the bathroom, but that's when I got called to get ready for a live inning.

At that moment, I thought, "Well, this is where I can see if I'm a pretender or if I can actually call a decent game." I went to Jake, who was calling for people, and he said I would be going in the 13th inning at the plate. Another guy came over, and he would be working the bases. So, I took my scrawny self over to where some shin guards and a chest protector were. I finally got them on, putting my umpire pants and a polo shirt on top. I didn't really get to see how I looked, but I felt like a real umpire, except I didn't have any tights with me, so the leg guards were up against my bare, hairy legs. Putting them on and adjusting all the straps was hard, but taking them off afterward was more challenging because I pulled some of the hair in the process.

But I think I did well. I brushed off the plate, got some baseballs in my ball bag, had my indicator ready, called play, and felt like I did a decent job. We both worked the entire 13th inning, and the break between half-innings was just 30 seconds or so, which was good. After that inning, I removed all the protective equipment and got ready to work the bases in the 15th inning. I felt like a real umpire.

When we finished, we went to the podium behind home plate to get our critiques. Mitch gave me mine, which I was very relieved about since he wasn't someone mean. He said that on the bases, when a fly ball is hit to left field with a runner on first, I should shade toward the ball, and if the ball is caught, shade back toward the runner. At the plate, there was a ball approaching out of play, and he said I need to get set before it settles so I can see it better. As far as I'm concerned, if those were my only two issues, I did way better than I thought I could. There are still five days left, but I may walk out of here and be able to manage a game after all.

Following innings, we cleaned everything up and met around podium three for end-of-day announcements and the strike three contest. The contest was called off after two guys in favor of a contestant who started his call. Then, a guy behind him handed him two beers that had just been opened and were gushing. He slapped them together and started chugging. Junior asked if any of the other contestants wanted to go after that one, and they said no, so that guy won today. We were then released, and I returned to the hotel room, where I took off sweaty clothes, cooled down, and ordered a stuffed crust pizza for my dinner.

January 26

Going into this week, I felt it would be trying. So far, it has been. We started at the fields, where it was humid, and I sweated a lot. I think I may have tied yesterday's record. After formation, we went into control games and cages. My crew started in the cage, doing simple stuff. After that, we had a control game that I did alright in (I'm getting better), then lunch (I got the country-fried steak special), and then finished up the last control game, where I was just baserunning. While waiting my turn, I noticed Junior and Jansen walking down from the podium toward the first base dugout. Jansen walked onto the field toward me. I had a slight feeling that they were aiming for me, but it turned out Jansen just got the helmet I was using and did some running himself. As he walked towards me, he put his hands up like he was asking for a ball, but then he reached up toward my head, so I held the brim of my cap while he pulled the helmet off.

Once that last control game was done, we started innings, and I decided to be the ball boy today because I was tired. During some innings, my crew got called for cages again, so I got someone else to take over as the ball boy and geared up for cage work. Mitch said the batter could do whatever he wanted except hit the ball—check swing, foul tip (we tap the bat with our hand to make the sound), swing and miss, and even argue some. Everyone decided to argue because baseball situations can be fun.

After we finished there, I returned to being the ball boy and rounded out the day with end-of-day announcements, the strike three contest, and a joke from Junior about a story I've heard before (and you may have too). He personalized it to sound like he and Jansen were at some of Joe West's land. It's basically this story:

Former New York Yankee manager Billy Martin tells a story about going to South Texas to deer hunt with Hall of Famer Mickey Mantle.

When they arrived at the ranch of one of Mantle's friends, Mickey said, "You stay in the car. I'll go in and talk to my buddy, and we'll go right out and hunt."

Once they exchanged greetings, the owner said, "Heck, Mickey, you can hunt all over my place, but would you do me a favor? I have a pet mule who's going blind, and I don't have the guts to kill the poor fellow. Would you kill him for me?" Mickey agreed, but decided to play a joke on Martin, coming out and slamming the door like he was mad.

When Billy asked what the problem was, Mickey said, "He won't let us hunt here."

"You've got to be kidding," said Martin.

"No, I'm not," fumed Mantle, "and I'm so mad that I'm going to go by the barn and shoot his mule."

"Mickey, you can't shoot that man's mule."

"The heck I can't," Mantle replied, "I'm gonna kill that mule."

Once they found the mule, Mickey took his rifle and POW, shot the mule dead. Turning around and seeing Martin's rifle smoking, Mantle asked, "What the heck are you doing?"

"I got three of his cows," answered Billy.

Saturday will be our last working day, with that evening being awards and a cookout. Sunday will be evaluations. Given all that, I plan to head home Sunday unless my evaluation is late or some other guys want me to stay. Even then, I can probably spend some time with them for a little while until I decide to hit the road. Six hours is a long drive, and I want to get home to rest, relax, and prepare for Universal Studios.

January 27

Innings. That's what we did today—innings. Okay, that's not everything. First, I had breakfast and then went to the fields, where we had roll call and formation. Then, we did innings all day. Not me, but a lot of people. I served as the ball boy again, and I suspect I'll get a couple of innings tomorrow (one as the plate umpire, one as the base umpire). We had cages running, and my crew had a turn today. Meatloaf was the lunch special, so I got that.

During Frank Jones's inning (someone in my crew), Hunter took an at-bat and watched three strikes down the pipe. Everyone thought Frank wouldn't get a job after ringing the boss man up, but Hunter didn't swing, so that's his fault. After strike three, Hunter drew a line in the dirt, and then Frank ejected him. If I get an inning tomorrow, I hope Junior comes up and strikes out so I can ring him up. Although he's been hitting well lately, I doubt he will strike out.

After everything was done, we had end-of-day announcements, including the strike three contest, ArRee's cookout, and singing "Happy Birthday" to Larry Garcia, whose birthday is Saturday. Hunter also reassured everyone, since some guys got concerned after hearing Junior's joke yesterday, that the story was "bulls***." He didn't want PETA getting onto them.

Apparently, today was ArRee's last day here because he has to go home to take care of something tomorrow. He told us he hates having to leave because we're like family to him (that's what umpire school does to many people), and I think we all feel the same way. He always had a loudspeaker for music during breaks and lunch and was always loud and energetic, especially in formation. He also will miss top tens, awards, and evaluations, so I know it hurts him, and it also does for us. He said he'd be back next year, and as of right now, I probably will be too. Hopefully, I'll see him again because he's a great guy.

We then hung out for a while near ArRee's RV, which he parked closer to the field for the cookout, even though there was the added risk of it being hit by a foul ball, but luckily that didn't happen. After a while, only a few of us left, and it started raining, so we packed it up and said our farewells to ArRee. He told me that I'm a stud, that he sees my energy on the field (which means something coming from him), and reiterated that I've got to believe it, along with some other reassuring stuff. I may have to add him to my list of people I think about when things get rough to keep me going. So far, I have three off the top of my head: my high school science teacher Mr. Boyer, ABO commissioner Taylor Duncan, and my old college church group leader Matt Law (if you're reading this, I hope to see you soon). There are some others as well that either fluctuate in and out of the list or that I don't see too often: my counselor Fred, a guy I met while filming for Central football named Jayson, my grandpa, the closest I've ever gotten to a brother in my friend Tucker, and even a guy I saw in the Publix parking lot one day when I was gathering some carts to take inside. As he was watching me, he said, "You're gonna do big things in life." I said thank you because he didn't have to take the time to say that to a young grocery bagger, and then he added, "As long as you're dedicated. A lot of kids your age—they're not dedicated." That may not seem like a lot, but when you've been working at the same place for a while, doing the same thing, and you get that feeling of monotony, all during the summer heat, words like that have a lasting effect, which is why I remembered them. I think ArRee would be an excellent addition to that list, particularly if I see him next year. That just goes to show that you never know who you can impact in a powerful way, so strive to be a positive person so that that's what sticks.

I've heard that umpire school brings people together, and I've felt the experience of being part of a group and having that camaraderie before, and that's exactly what's happened here. As I said before, I plan on leaving after my evaluation on Sunday, but I'll probably spend some time with some guys before I head out. This year's class has been one of the smallest, if not the smallest, of any year of umpire school, so there's been more opportunity to form bonds and relationships with fellow students and instructors. That's a big part of life—people. I always try to be someone others say positive things about and who makes others feel better about themselves or their actions. Essentially, I want to be for others what those other people I mentioned are for me. I've been told I've done those things plenty of times, but I know I'm not finished meeting people, so the work is never done. That's also why I try to maintain my current relationships with those I already know because they just might be the ones to introduce me to or recommend me to someone who either can make an impact on me, or that I can make an impact on.

Anyway, enough with all that spiritual, emotional stuff. I'm going to eat dinner now and prepare for a likely inning tomorrow (assuming the fields are dry).

January 28

Today started in an interesting way. When I got up to get breakfast, I ran into a lady in the elevator who seemed anxious. She was headed to the basement while I was going to the lobby. She muttered to herself, "I hate elevators. I hate people," which struck me as odd. I understand some people don't like elevators, but disliking people? That's harder for me to grasp. It makes you think about how some people struggle with social interactions and how prevalent those feelings might be.

Breakfast was the usual: eggs, bacon, and a waffle, and it never disappoints. During the end-of-day announcements, Hunter mentioned feedback about the meal plans from our questionnaires. Personally, I have no issues with the meals.

We started the day in the classroom because the instructors wanted to touch on a couple of things, such as roll call and announcing innings inside, which is easier. They also discussed the importance of our end-of-school surveys and encouraged us to provide honest feedback rather than just saying everything was good. It's refreshing how straightforward and honest the Wendelstedt Umpire School staff is, unlike the usual sugarcoating we get from most places.

We then went to the fields, where four crews were involved in control games on field 1, and three crews, including mine, did pause-read-react drills down the first baseline. After that, we started innings, and just as I predicted, I had one today. I partnered with a guy named Shaun (finally, someone whose name is spelled sensibly). I had the plate for the 6th inning and the bases for the 8th, and I did alright. Tom Fornarola gave me feedback about being louder and more aggressive behind the plate. I usually don't have that issue, but innings can be stressful, and I naturally get anxious.

After today, we have two more working days—tomorrow and Saturday, which will also be awards day. Sunday will be evaluations, and then I'll head back home. They're moving my roommate Xavier to a room with another guy who's leaving the same day he is, and Frank Jones will be coming to my room since we're both leaving on Sunday. Since today was my last full day with Xavier, he showed me some photos of his family that he keeps in his wallet.

Things are winding down, and it won't be long before I'll be making the long trek back to Phenix City, reflecting on my progress and experiences here, and considering what to do with my new abilities after the Universal trip. I'll never forget this experience, from the scenery to the material learned, the people, the food, and everything in between. I appreciate every day here because I am sure that I will wish I was back in just a few short months or weeks. It'll be interesting to get settled back home and feel like I'm somewhere different, but at the same time, like I never left. I hope people will be excited to see me when I return because a month away from home is a long time.

We did innings for the rest of the day with a lunch break in the middle, and many instructors still batted in the innings, which everyone enjoyed. We finished the day with end-of-day announcements and the strike three contest. Hunter reminded us to let them know if we have any legal issues or marks on our record to avoid problems with leagues that play in Canada, as Canada doesn't allow US felons.

I'll probably start packing up some things and putting them in the car in the next day or so to make Sunday easier. It's been fun here, and I know I'll have plenty of tales to share from this month-long journey that not many others can say they've taken.

January 29

Hunter told us at the end of the day's announcements that we had completed the last full working day of umpire school. Tomorrow will start in the classroom. Then we'll head to the fields to even up the number of innings everyone has, so I'll most likely get another one. After that, we'll have a cookout, marking the end of our activities at the fields.

As usual, I started the day with breakfast, but only after helping Xavier move his luggage to another room. I enjoyed sharing a room with him. As always, we began our work with formation and cage work for my crew. I think this will be my last cage session of umpire school. We had innings all day, though I didn't participate. Jansen reminded us that no one is guaranteed a job recommendation, so my inning tomorrow could be crucial. I've been telling myself it's okay if I don't get selected because I've enjoyed the experience here. However, I also remember why I came: to get an opportunity to work on a baseball field and make a living, rather than going back to a customer service job with a passive-aggressive team leader.

Lunch was baked ziti, after which we took a class picture on the nearby football field stands. I'm curious to see what they'll do with it. During innings, the Wendelstedt Umpire School merchandise table was set up for the last time. Next to it was a booth for an electronic indicator, a tool umpires use to keep track of balls, strikes, and outs. The electronic version had a small screen and was still in its early stages. The final product will cost around $100, be waterproof, and have a colored screen. Louis, the representative from Umpire Stuff, gave us small green keychains for 50% off an indicator, only available to Wendelstedt graduates of 2021. If I decide to get one, I can buy it for $50. If I find a red keychain in the package, I can get a refund and the indicator for free.

When the final products are ready, I plan to get one in March or April. I could get a prototype next week for $79.99, but I'll wait for the final version. Being one of the first umpires in my area to have one is exciting. I've only met one other Wendelstedt graduate from my area, a guy I saw at Publix wearing a Wendelstedt beanie.

We also had the strike three contest, and there will be a final one tomorrow with all the winners. The top tens will be announced tomorrow, which will be interesting. Everyone wants me to participate because I've created a lot of good material. Sweet vengeance is coming the instructors' way, especially Junior. It is a fitting climax to an action-packed month.

Frank just got here as I'm writing this, and I will probably hang out with some other guys before and after dinner. I learned yesterday that the guy who cooks our breakfast and dinner used to be a professional umpire until he got fired. His last name is Rackley. His brother, David Rackley, is a current MLB umpire. I remember him because he was the home plate umpire for a Phillies-Braves game I attended on July 30th, 2016.

I've found interesting tidbits at every corner, and I hope there will be a few more in the next two days. Tomorrow is our last working day, and Sunday will be evaluations before I return home. I can't decide if I'm ready to be back home. It'll be good to return to familiarity, but this month-long escape from reality has been a wild ride—one that I'll never forget.

January 30

I woke up with a different roommate and went to get breakfast for the final time. After eating and getting ready for the day, Frank gave me some pointers on my umpire appearance, including the New Balance base shoes he gave me last night. Earlier in the course, I noticed how snug his umpire shirts were, and some other guys said he gets them tailored. This was proven true when he suggested that I hold my arm out, grab the part of the sleeve that hangs down under the arm, and have a tailor clip it so the sleeve fits closer.

We started in the classroom with the top ten roast session. The instructors went first, with Ben handling their part. The theme was "Top Ten Students Who Make Us Shake Our Heads." ArRee Bateman was said to have "come to umpire school to be a better umpire and left a better DJ," which sounded more like a compliment. Ryan Haswell was told that after umpire school, he was needed back at the North Pole, suggesting he looks like an elf.

You may remember that in the first week when discussing hit-by-pitches, I asked a question using an example from a stickball game where I leaned my knees into a pitch and disguised it as my stride. Junior then dubbed me a cheater for the remainder of the course, though he reassured me it wasn't meant maliciously. Today, Ben reminded everyone of that, saying, "Samuel Barrett, the cheater who apologized to the game of baseball..." Then Junior said he had spoken to those in power (figuratively speaking) and they were going to pardon me. He pulled out a framed pardon, which they had typed up, made to look professional, printed, and framed. It was ridiculous and funny. Junior and I then took a picture with it. Later, when I took another photo with him, he asked if I had it. I said yes, and he said, "Good. Never leave home without it." I'll certainly never leave home without that memory.

After that, the students had their chance to roast the instructors. Someone back home had told me not to do it and just respect the instructors, and I gave it a little thought. But after the pardon, I knew all bets were off. My turn was absolutely expected, not only to humor everyone else but to defend my pride. It was established early on that I would go last since everyone speculated my material would be the best. When Junior asked if anyone else had anything, no one responded, he looked at me and said, "You ready, Sam?" I nodded and made my way to the front podium. The next ten minutes were filled with lethal burns, roasts, and hysterical laughter. I began by praising God, then went in:

"I GUESS I'LL START WITH TOM HANAHAN, WHO'S A BROWNS FAN...HE DID THAT TO HIMSELF.

SO I GUESS I'LL MOVE ON TO REED, WHO, LIKE TOM, LOOKS LIKE HE'S BEEN JACKING OFF TOO MUCH. KEEP HIM AWAY FROM ALLY (an employee at the hotel who a lot of guys had eyes for). THAT'S PROBABLY WHY ALL THE INSTRUCTORS GOT AN AIRBNB THIS YEAR-SHE'S PROBABLY GOT RESTRAINING ORDERS AGAINST Y'ALL.

YEAH, REED LOOKS LIKE THE TESTOSTERONE BEN HASN'T DEVELOPED YET. OUR DEFENSE DROPS MORE BALLS THAN BEN HAS AT THIS POINT.

MOVING ON FROM BALLS, LET'S TALK ABOUT DICKS. LIKE JAKE (Bruner), WHOSE HEAD LOOKS LIKE A FRESHLY-CIRCUMCISED DICK. OF COURSE, HE'S NOT THE ONLY ONE...

JANSEN, GO AHEAD. STOP FLEXING AND TAKE OFF YOUR MLB HAT. YEP, THERE'S THAT MR. CLEAN HEAD. JANSEN THINKS WE'LL BE IMPRESSED BY HIS MLB STUFF...(Impersonating Jansen speaking into a megaphone) "BUT THAT'S NOT WHAT HAPPENS. JUST LIKE A PICKOFF PLAY, JANSEN IN THE BED HAPPENS EXTREMELY FAST."

OK, I'LL GO CLEAN NOW. SO I'LL TALK ABOUT TOM FORNOROLA, OR "COOL TOM." I'VE GOT A GOOD IMPRESSION OF HIM; YOU WANNA HEAR IT? (Impersonating Tom's Italian-sounding voice) "OK, SO WHEN YOU'RE THE BASE UMPIRE, MAKE SURE TO DROP-STEP WITH YOUR LEFT FOOT, BUT DON'T GET SUCKED INTO THE PLAY. KEEP YOUR CHEST SQUARE TO THE BASEBALL." NOW LET'S TALK ABOUT WHO WE'VE ALL BEEN WAITING FOR ME TO TALK ABOUT.

LET'S TALK ABOUT JUNIOR, WHO LOOKS LIKE HE SITS ON HIS FRONT PORCH AND WATCHES BUSES RUN OVER KIDS. IT'S PROBABLY BEST THAT THOSE KIDS DIE SO THEY DON'T HAVE TO SEE JUNIOR'S SLENDERMAN FACE. DEREK (Stevenson, who is gay) IS STRAIGHTER THAN JUNIOR'S FEET WHEN HE WALKS. AND I'M CLEARLY FUNNIER THAN JUNIOR'S LAME JOKES. THAT'S PROBABLY WHAT JOE GIRARDI THOUGHT OF HIM. HE SAID WE SHOULD ACT LIKE WE HAVE THE BIGGEST DICK ON THE FIELD, EVEN THOUGH HE DOESN'T. WELL, HE'S RIGHT BECAUSE HE'S PROBABLY GOT A SHRIMP.

SPEAKING OF SHRIMP, I WANNA GIVE A SHOUT-OUT TO JAMES (an instructor who came down for the second week). I

HOPE THE SHRIMPIN' BUSINESS IS GOIN' GOOD FOR HIM (said impersonating Bubba from FORREST GUMP). WAIT, HE'S NOT HERE. WELL, WHERE IS HE? (Alex Schumaker then says, "I gotta find Bubba!" then I drop everything and run out the door)."

Once that ended, we had a Q&A session to ask the instructors, including the MLB umpires, any questions about umpire stuff. Quite a few guys had questions, and once those were all answered, we headed to the fields for another first-base call game. Jake used his megaphone to call out innings as we walked down. Since most people had had three innings by this point and I'd only had two, I suspected I'd get one, and sure enough, I was the first name called. As I walked over, Jake looked back at me twice and said, "I didn't like the head penis joke." I didn't know what to say until he reassured me he was just kidding.

For the first base "whacker" drill, we were split into two groups—base umpires and runners. The group of umpires tried to get as many calls right as they could, then we'd switch to runners, and the other group would have their chance. Both groups tied, so we had a sudden death round where two umpires from each group would take a turn, and whoever got a call right or wrong first would determine the winner. The instructors picked our sudden death umpire, and Junior picked me. Reggie from the other group went first and got his call right, so I had to get mine right to avoid our group doing formation. The first baseman tagged the runner. I called him out on the tag, but Tom, acting as the first baseman, showed me the ball in his bare hand and an empty mitt. Junior asked what the first baseman had tagged the runner with, and I said the ball, he asked where the ball was, and I mistakenly said the glove. We lost. We did formation, had our last lunch (I got the special of pulled pork and beans), and then I got ready for my last piece of work—a live inning. I had the plate in the first inning and the bases in the third. Despite my chest protector being a little loose because I hurried, I killed that inning. I even questioned a wood bat I hadn't seen before to keep the game fair. On the bases, I felt like I slipped up a couple of times, but my only critiques were minor. If my only issue was timing, then I crushed it today.

After that, I finally let go of all my nerves. From the top tens this morning to the first base call to my inning, it was a pretty stressful beginning. But I started hitting my stride in the live innings, even though someone cracked that wood bat. Once the innings ended, we completed the Wendelstedt Umpire School curriculum. We had a small ceremony where we received our diplomas, took pictures with the MLB umpires, and stood around the diamond for a big class picture. We had our final end-of-day announcements and special awards, though I didn't receive any. We then had the final strike three contest with all the winners, and a guy from our crew won. Hunter said, "And just like that, it's over." Dang.

We have evaluations in the classroom tomorrow morning starting at nine, but we're done with the fields. We had dinner outside, talked, took pictures, and eventually returned to the hotel. I will probably hang out with my friends here one more time tonight (assuming they don't have any more random girls in the room like last night) and pack some things to put in the car. That way, I can get up, get ready, check out of the hotel, get my evaluation done in the classroom, and then head back home tomorrow morning. It's really been fun here. I've thoroughly enjoyed this escape from reality for a month, and now it's all pretty much over.

January 31

I started today by waking up, but we had no breakfast, so I took my time getting up and getting ready. While Frank was still in bed, I got dressed in my charcoal grey suit with a blue and silver striped tie to look my best for the final day of umpire school evaluations. I wasn't as stressed about the evaluations as the drive home and ensuring I had everything. After packing up, checking out, and arriving at the classroom, I could focus on saying farewell to the people I met and on the evaluation.

Last night, Ben posted a spreadsheet on Google Classroom where we could sign up for our evaluation time slots. I chose 11 a.m. as the closest available spot, but there were a few times when someone would erase another person's name and put their own, which was pretty messed up. Eventually, we sorted it all out.

When we got to the classroom and started talking, the instructors began calling us one by one through the vault door that led to the other half of the classroom, sealed off by a retractable wall. When my turn came up, Tom called me in. I went to the table closest to the door where he and Junior were waiting. Junior first told me my score, which was 219 out of 250 on the tests. He said it wasn't bad, but I could do better, which is true— some guys had scores in the 240s—so I should stay in the rulebook.

Then came the moment everyone at umpire school waits for: finding out if you got selected for a job recommendation. Well, did I?

Yes. Yes, I did.

They will be recommending me for a league this summer. Junior asked if I would accept, and of course, I said yes, adding that it would be nice if it were close to home. After telling him where home was for me, he said there wasn't anywhere close, but that didn't affect my decision. It didn't hurt to bring it up. He congratulated me and said someone named John White, whom I might have met earlier in the course, would call or email me at some point to discuss the job further.

Junior mentioned that the biggest thing I needed to work on was my confidence in my motions, such as awards of bases, which can be hard when starting because you must remember everything. He said if I ever needed anything, I should contact them. That was it. I shook hands with Tom and Junior, who congratulated me again, including on the pardon.

After that, I said my final goodbyes to some of the guys, headed to a gas station, and got on the road. It was a long trip, and it started raining in north Florida, but I made it back to Phenix City, Alabama, where I'm writing this now. I've unpacked a lot, will wash a bunch of stuff, and pick through the bag of street clothes that I barely touched to see what I can leave packed for the Universal trip. On the third, my family will head that way.

This past month has been one of the most memorable experiences of my life. The perfect combination of fun, stress, and competition made it not only enjoyable but productive as well. I will never forget the start of my umpire career, which looks like it might have some substance to it. Perhaps this is the start of my own road to the show. So y'all go ahead and play it on the PlayStation—I might get to live it.

EXPEDITION LEAGUE

April 23

I'll be in the summer college Expedition League from late May to mid-August. John White and a few other guys from umpire school are placing me there this year. My partner didn't attend this year but did last year. We're getting pretty much everything covered: two caps (another baseball term—"cap" instead of "hat"), two black short-sleeve uniform shirts (my partner and I are also getting a light blue shirt and a long-sleeve black shirt, as those are optional), and a light jacket with zip-off sleeves. They also provide round-trip transportation for our first game and home once the season ends, pre- and post-game meals, travel reimbursement (my partner will receive it since he'll be driving), and hotel accommodations.

I do need to buy at least a pair of plate pants (the kind they prefer us to have), warm-weather tights, a big equipment bag, and a few other things.

So, there's a lot to prepare for, but I also have some exciting events coming up. My dad and I are taking a trip to Texas so I can learn how to navigate an airport since I've never been on a plane before. The only time I've really been to an airport was in December when then-Vice President Mike Pence visited Columbus, GA. We'll visit Houston, San Antonio, and Austin, which should be a fun experience.

May 24

I thought umpire school was daunting. I woke up at six this morning to finish getting ready to fly out to Caldwell, Idaho, my first stop in the Expedition League. My parents drove me up to Atlanta, parked, walked me in, and got my two big bags checked. They walked with me through the security line until it started to twist and turn, and then we had to part ways. If everything goes as planned, I won't see them, anyone else in my family, or my friends until early August. Gosh, that's too long.

Somehow, I navigated through the Atlanta, Salt Lake City, and Boise airports, and my partner picked me up at the latter to take me to the hotel. He's out getting some food, so I figured this would be a good time to write without him getting curious.

I received my uniforms today except for the long-sleeved black and light blue shirts. A couple of months ago, when I went to pay for them online, the website said those were out of stock. When I contacted Purchase Officials, our uniform supplier, they said they took those shirts off the website to ensure the Northwoods League umpires would get theirs but assured me that my order would be fulfilled. Well, apparently not. Even if I contact someone about it now, where would they send it? We will be switching hotels so often that it would be a shot in the dark. They could send it to a ballpark where I will be soon. I hope the timing works out, but it would still be a hassle. I guess we just won't be wearing blue this year.

Everything else looks good, though. I got my number choice of 37 correct, and my cap choices of a fitted four-stitch and a fitted six-stitch. The stitch count refers to the number of stitches you see on the brim. If you take a cap and count the number of rows of stitching on the brim, most have eight. Umpire caps have fewer, typically six on the bases and four behind the plate, allowing the mask to be put on and removed easily.

May 25

Opening Day for the Expedition League umpire crew A, which is mine. My crew partner is Jake Al-Mazroa. He's nice enough and pretty relaxed. I'm glad I won't have to deal with a maniac all summer.

Yesterday, with it being the first game for us and both teams (The Mining City Tommyknockers and Canyon County Spuds are both new entries in the league), us being the youngest umpire crew in the league (and me not only looking like but also being the youngest umpire in the league), the quality of baseball not being great, and the fact that it rained earlier in the day (but we were still able to have a game because the infield is artificial turf), I'll grade my Opening Day as average. That may seem kind of low, so I'll expand:

A runner attempted to steal third at one point, and in the two-man system, it can be difficult to get over to third quickly enough to get a better look. I called the runner safe because that's what I saw (though Jake said I didn't make any call. I hope he was wrong). The runner then went off the base (though I don't know whether that was because he thought he was out or if his momentum took him off the base), but before I made an out call, I wanted to check with my partner, so I did, and after he simply said, "Call him out," I did. The problem is, we didn't call time before doing that. Nothing else happened, but that's just a simple fix for next time.

Another situation occurred in a double play when the out was made at second base, and then the throw went to first. I don't remember if the runner beat the ball or not, but I do remember that the runner missed first base. I called the runner safe because

(I assumed) I had the runner beating the ball to the base. The visiting team assistant coach then came out wanting me to get help, so I did because I felt like I may have messed it up, but according to my partner, I didn't because since he missed the base, that must be appealed, so the runner was safe. The coach was still upset though, telling us to...well I'll keep this family-friendly, but it resulted in Jake ejecting him because everyone could hear it.

There was a home run during the game, and I couldn't see the ball as it soared over the outfield, so I relied on the thud of the scoreboard (and the batter watching the ball after he hit it) to confirm that it was a home run. That was cool.

After the game, we went back into our dressing room, where Jake called Mitch Messer, our supervisor, about the ejection, and he told us that we did fine, but that the quality of baseball was not good. We'll see how it is tomorrow when I have the plate.

What is our dressing room like in Caldwell's Wolfe Field? There's a structure underneath the grandstand that has the women's restroom on the near side and the men's on the far side. We go through the men's door and through the restroom into another door that leads to a small room with a big sink at one end and bunches of boxes of baseballs on the other. Not too big, but it feels kind of cozy and protected from the outside. Here's hoping some guys don't wait outside our door in the men's restroom to mug us.

The Spuds' manager, Sean Walsh, does a lot for the team, from managing the team to coordinating concessions and souvenir sales to tending to us. I hope we don't have to eject him and then after the game have to have him do something for us.

That'd be awkward, but if he refused, we'd just call Mitch and the situation would likely be diffused fairly quickly.

On the way to the ballpark, I saw two speed limit road signs that interested me: the first one said, "35 unless otherwise posted," and the second one came right after, and it said the speed limit was 45. So I guess the 45 is the "otherwise posted" part.

My first-ever nine-inning game behind the plate is tomorrow. I've done two seven-inning games in one day before, but not this. My nerves are high.

May 26

My strike zone throughout the night was pretty good. Obviously, fans would disagree, but that's part of the job. I had my first ejection of the season, so two games in, two ejections for crew A. Walsh was coaching third base when I rang up a Spuds batter on strikes. Walsh didn't like it, and since this wasn't the first ball/strike issue I'd had with him, this time was enough to run him.

There weren't any close plays on the plate, so that was good. There were some hecklers in the stands during the game. The first one directed at me was some guys asking, "Left hand for pancakes, right hand for waffles." I didn't respond because I figured I should stay professional but because I like both. Later on, they became more confrontational, making fun of my youth by calling me a kid and saying, "It's past your bedtime." They also poked fun at my physique, saying, "If I didn't know any better, I'd have thought you were a bodybuilder with all that muscle" and "It's okay to eat a cheeseburger every now and then" (I actually eat a lot of those, by the way). I didn't take too much offense to the humor. It's the fans who think they know the game and how to officiate better than those who have been trained and are positioned on the field that I have a problem with.

The last three innings were physically the toughest. I believe it was in the top of the seventh when a ball either bounced into the inside of my right shin guard or hit it flush. I took a moment to walk it off, but it still hurts, and I have a knot there. In the ninth, a ball was fouled off right to my right shoulder, which also hurt and still does, but there's no mark there. A ball was fouled straight to my mask the next at-bat and knocked it sideways. It didn't hurt, but it did knock my head in a different direction, which I guess happens when a ball gets fouled off straight back by a college player. I didn't take a moment that time because it didn't hurt, and there were two outs in the ninth. The silver lining of those hits is that they shut up the hecklers for a bit.

Fortunately, I had two nice catchers to talk with, and they were both respectful and understanding of the crowd. The Tommyknockers catcher rotates throwing down between innings. Usually, after the last warm-up pitch, the catcher catches it and throws to second base, but the Tommyknockers catcher would throw to third one inning, then second the next, then first the next. Interesting.

So today, I have the bases, and then tomorrow we get up really early for our ten-hour drive to Casper, Wyoming, where I will start the series behind the plate. Here's hoping every game and series won't be like this one. Otherwise, this will be a long summer (or a short one if the league decides to replace us with two older guys, but I don't think that would happen. If it did, it probably wouldn't happen until after the All-Star break).

High-scoring games take longer, so 16-9 took over four

hours. So anyways, so far...hopefully we're getting all the rough games out of the way now.

May 27

I had the bases, and while this game lasted a little longer than our first one, it went a lot smoother. There weren't any bad calls, and a manager only came out to discuss a call once, but I feel like I got it right. The home Spuds got their first-ever franchise win, and when Jake and I walked off the field, we smiled at each other. He said, "Good job." We had said before the game that we didn't want any ejections, and we didn't have any. All around, it was a good game for us. Here's hoping we can keep that momentum and have all our games go like that.

When I'm on the bases here in Caldwell, as I'm running around the field, I can smell and even feel the stench of pee in the air. I don't know where it's coming from—maybe cows come around and pee behind the outfield wall near the railroad track— but it almost felt like I was getting out of a dirty pool.

Jake had a good plate game, and tonight I'll get my turn in the first game in Casper, Wyoming. We have another game tomorrow, followed by two days off—the only time this season we have that, so I'll be sure to do some laundry then. After those two days, we have three more games in Casper before heading to Minot, North Dakota. The good thing is, after Minot, we go to Dickinson, ND. Most of the teams are in Mountain Time, but there are a couple in Central Time, so when I get to those places, I may try to convince myself that I'm simply in Auburn instead of halfway across the country.

After a ten-hour drive, we'll be in Wyoming, and the game

time is 6:35 instead of 7:05. I'm sure all three people in Wyoming will make for a decent crowd.

May 30

On our travel day last Friday, we were supposed to have a game that evening here in Casper. However, on the way, we were notified that the Tommyknockers (the visiting team for this series, coincidentally our previous series) had their bus break down, causing them to arrive in Casper yesterday instead of the day before. As a result, instead of a game on Friday and one yesterday, we had a doubleheader yesterday, with two seven-inning games. I was totally fine with that, as I've handled those multiple times during high school season.

When Jake and I were informed about the schedule change, we relaxed and figured as long as we could take care of the broken mirror issue, everything would be fine. Before we knew about the rescheduling, Sean from the Spuds sent us a message saying he had received a call from the Fairfield hotel where they had put us, reporting a broken mirror in room 228, which was ours, after we had left. I vaguely recalled seeing it, but I definitely didn't cause it. I asked Jake since he had arrived at the room before I had, and he confirmed he had seen the broken mirror when he arrived. I'm not sure what, if anything, will come of that, but hopefully, it won't reflect negatively on us since we weren't responsible for it.

I had the plate for the first game, and it went very smoothly, aside from a long, high-scoring top of the seventh inning. Apart from that, the pitching was good, though the Horseheads probably should have won that game because their pitcher was performing exceptionally well and was very quick (I believe he was adhering to the twelve-second rule between pitches, which is the official rule, not twenty seconds). After that game, Jake and I had just twenty minutes to change and prepare for the second game, which I worked the bases for. That game also went smoothly, ending in a one-run game. Literally, the Tommyknockers scored one run in the first inning, and that was it; their pitcher was lights out.

After the games, we changed into our regular clothes, gathered all the food the young Horseheads attendants provided us before, between, and after the games, and then returned to the car to return to the hotel. It was a good night.

May 31

The boredom here is driving me insane. Nothing else has happened since I arrived in Wyoming. My partner and I stay on opposite sides of the room and don't speak until it's time to leave for a game. Yesterday was incredibly dull, and today doesn't look any better. I've even run out of food except for a bag of sour cream and onion chips, and there's nowhere decent within walking distance to get more. Looks like I might be malnourished all summer.

June 1

I'm returning to the hotel room after umpiring the plate this evening. The game went well, clocking in at under three hours. There were a couple of tough fair/foul calls and some checked swings, not to mention the usual strike zone discrepancies, but those are par for the course. You might wonder, "How can a fair/foul decision be difficult?" Unless you've been through the training at the premier umpire school like Tom Hanahan's, you wouldn't understand. When multiple fielders are diving for a ball, they can obscure where it lands, complicating the call. In one instance, I ruled foul. The Sabre Dogs' manager motioned from the third base coach's box that he wanted to discuss it, and I welcomed the conversation. He asked for my perspective, and I explained what I saw. To my surprise, he calmly responded, "It was fair, but you're doing great," with a smile. His graciousness took me aback; he wasn't confrontational at all. I acknowledged his comment and moved on, hoping for a favorable outcome for his team. They ended up winning 7-3.

I also took another hit to my right shin, right where I was hit last week. Ouch, it still hurts. The bruise from last week's impact was just starting to fade. Darn it.

June 3

Yesterday, I was on the bases for a reasonably okay game. I did make a mistake on a check swing call because I was battling the sun, but it was clear that the Horseheads hitter had gone around. I incorrectly called it a no-swing when Jake pointed to me for the appeal. Being understanding, the Sabre Dogs' manager chewed me out from the dugout, and I let him voice his objection. I believe in fairness; if I mess up a call, it's only right that others have the chance to express their disagreement. Besides that, I handled some close calls at second and third well.

At the plate, Jake called a runner safe after he touched home plate before being tagged. However, the Horsehead's manager argued that the runner should be out because he didn't slide. This is not a rule requirement, contrary to his belief.

Overall, the game ran a bit longer than we would have preferred, but we managed through it.

Tonight, I'll be umpiring behind the plate before an early start tomorrow, heading to Minot, North Dakota, home of the Sabre Dogs. I hope for another game under three hours with minimal (or no) issues. At least I'll start with the bases in the first game in Minot.

June 4

Coming into yesterday's game, I knew that both teams, Jake and myself, were traveling after the game. Being behind the plate for that game, I understood that the pace of the game somewhat depended on me, so my goal was to keep everything smooth and moving. And for the most part, that's what happened......until suddenly it didn't.

Sure, some were complaining about the strike zone, but let me clarify: a hitter heading toward first base doesn't automatically make it ball four. Plus, players with bad body language aren't doing themselves any favors. It's challenging to determine if a pitch hitting the hands area hit the hands or the bat knob, and there were a few of those instances last night, which added a few extra minutes to the game.

However, the biggest eruption came after a wild pitch with a runner on third. The Horsehead's catcher retrieved the ball, threw it to the pitcher covering home, and clearly beat the runner. All I needed to do was see the tag and call him out.

I didn't see a tag. I called him safe. If you recall the Pirates/Braves game in 2011 with a similar play at the plate, you can guess what happened next.

The Horseheads manager stormed out, hurling spit and baseless insults. I ejected him, unfazed, because I saw the space between the mitt and the runner's leg.

The game ended with a lopsided score of 23-1, as the Horseheads resorted to a position player pitching in the 9th inning. Despite the score, I maintained my consistent strike zone (gotta uphold the integrity of the game). Eventually, the game concluded, and I returned the baseballs to the home dugout. One of their players, a catcher known for his complaints, had the audacity to tell me I didn't belong near their dugout. Considering they just lost by 22 runs, I wonder if he belongs in a college dugout. As we were leaving, one of their coaches offered us some pointless advice, which I dismissed. Perhaps I should have ejected them post-game.

Tonight, I'll be on the bases for our first game in Minot, kicking off our only series of the season there before heading to Dickinson, North Dakota, for two games and returning to Casper. I hope for a smoother experience in Minot; their coaches are pleasant, the ballpark looks appealing, and a change of scenery could be refreshing.

June 6

I've had two games in the past couple of days, one in each position. The game on the bases went fairly well. The Sabre Dogs' manager, Alex, came out to dispute a judgment call at first base, where I called the runner out, but he believed he was safe. He's been respectful overall, so I've tolerated a bit more from him. Being familiar from our previous Casper series, the whole team greets me by name when I step onto the field. I'm unsure if I should feel okay about that, but I do. Their first baseman, Beau Brewer, who's batting over .500 this season, looks remarkably like my best friend Tucker, except with facial hair, long hair, and eyes spaced farther apart.

Despite the game going well, I felt unusually stressed and out of place. Perhaps the nine-hour ride from Casper earlier in the day played a part, but honestly, this is becoming tough, and I question how much I'm enjoying it. Sure, it's baseball, but the constant travel, standing on the field for hours without a dugout to rest in, dealing with clueless fans, overly aggressive coaches, and egotistical players—it all wears on you, no matter how thick your skin. Yesterday, while trying to relax at the hotel, I suddenly couldn't catch my breath fully and felt chest pain, even though I wasn't physically active. I shared this with my family over the phone, and they told me about some pills hidden in one of my travel bags. I took one and eventually managed to sleep. Still, I remained uncertain about what was happening—whether it was a heart attack, panic attack, or just a physical manifestation of stress. I'm inclined to think it was stress-related.

Tomorrow, I'll be joining a different crew. It seems the league decided that having two of the youngest umpires in their first major traveling league together might not be the best idea. My new partner will be Tristyn, who's 38 years old. I'm open to this change, hoping it lifts my spirits and leads to more good games.

On the 5th, I was behind the plate for an okay game. Still, I received complaints from both sides, particularly the visiting Sasquatch manager, who continually disputed the strike zone. He claimed he wasn't trying to get ejected, so I didn't oblige (though that alone doesn't guarantee immunity from ejection). Oh well, they won by a run anyway.

During breaks between innings, entertainers from an organization called Zooperstars visited. They dress up sports stars as zoo animals (like Tommy Laswordfish and Tim Tebull). One entered our dressing room (not in costume), explained their act, and asked for our cooperation during the game. We agreed, and afterward, he gave us twenty dollars to split. Jake handed me two five-dollar bills—end of story. Their performances were amusing. During the Tim Tebull act, which dragged a bit, some fans urged me to eject him as he left the field, but I wasn't about to. I'm all for entertainment.

The game concluded after the Sasquatch scored in the 9th inning to take a one-run lead. The Sabre Dogs couldn't respond in the bottom half, so we retired to the umpires' room—a space adorned with framed photos and articles about local umpires, equipped with a fridge, lockers, and couches. The floor might be uneven, but it's still pretty cool.

June 8

I mentioned a couple of days ago that there would be a change in crew partners, but I didn't elaborate much. As you might recall, my previous partner was Jake, but the league decided having two 20-year-olds in the same crew wasn't the best idea, so now I'm paired with Tristyn, who's 35.

My initial thoughts on Tristyn? He's more outgoing than Jake, which makes him optimistic, and he provides constructive feedback when needed. I liked Jake because we both kept things simple off the field, but I'm also starting to appreciate Tristyn's approach. Our first noteworthy event together was when he got pulled over for speeding. Tristyn remained composed, and the officer was friendly. Apparently, in South Dakota, it's customary for the person to sit in the cop car to streamline processing. While Tristyn sorted things out with the officer, I found myself alone in the car, again in unfamiliar territory. It feels like a world away from any semblance of a stable daily life.

Tristyn is fun to be around. We've already visited and toured the South Dakota state capitol and plan to explore the Badlands this evening. That's more than I did on off days with Jake. I've worked two games with Tristyn so far—once on the bases and once behind the plate—and both were good, especially the game behind the plate, which was under three hours. That's always a plus. I think working with Tristyn will be a positive experience. It almost feels like being traded, in a way.

Here's a little fun fact: it's not uncommon for umpires to request team merchandise, typically caps when visiting different ballparks. Another umpire did this during my high school season in Reeltown, Alabama, and Tristyn has collected several caps from the Northwoods League, including his Traverse City Pit Spitters hat. I haven't done this yet, and I'm not sure if I will.

June 9

With Tristyn, things are feeling a bit better now. Tomorrow, I'll be on the bases in Sioux Falls as we follow both their Sun Fish and Pierre's Trappers for four games. Spending much of our season in the Dakotas, particularly in Pierre and Sioux Falls, I think developing a routine will be easier with this schedule.

Today was our off day, and despite the league scheduling us to travel on our next game days, Tristyn and I decided to make the most of it. We had lunch, and then in the evening, we visited the Badlands National Park, where we saw some breathtaking scenery and encountered various animals like prairie dogs, deer, sheep, and bison. The elevation made me a bit uneasy, but it was an experience. Looking up pictures of the area, you'll notice perfectly straight horizontal lines etched across the rocks. How that natural phenomenon occurred remains a mystery to me, but it was fascinating to witness up close.

As we were driving out to grab a meal at Subway before heading back to Sioux Falls, Tristyn, who had been hoping to spot some bison, remarked, "I wish we had seen some bison." I glanced out my window and asked, "You mean those bison?" He looked out my window, exclaimed, "Oh sh*t," and promptly pulled over to capture some photos.

Realizing it was late at Subway, I inquired about their leftover cookies, secretly hoping to snag some. The young employee nonchalantly replied, "We just leave them in here," as he casually rested his hand on the cookie display. If they're left out, how do they manage to stay so soft?

June 10

There were three games with Tristyn, and all three were good ones. Yesterday evening, before my game on the bases, the first thing that caught my attention was the scratchy sound system. The PA announcer sounded like he was speaking from a fish tank, though I doubt that was intentional (who are we kidding). There was a close call at first base where I called the runner safe, but Pierre's manager came out and politely requested an appeal. Tristyn and I conferred, and he decided to overturn my call, which cleared up the situation smoothly. Those calls can be tricky, even the routine ones, especially when you're in the middle of the infield with runners on base. Aside from that, it was an enjoyable game. There weren't many fans in attendance. The infield was artificial turf, a Sunfish player used a light blue bat, a foul ball shattered a bulb in a light tower (the sound was unmistakable), and the game finished in 2 hours and 32 minutes, which is always a plus. It could have been a tad quicker, but I'm not complaining.

Tonight, I'll be behind the plate, and I'm hoping for a repeat of my plate game in Pierre—a smooth and efficient game would be very welcome.

June 11

Last night's plate game had its moments, but it could have been smoother. We encountered some unusual situations. During a swinging strikeout, the catcher failed to catch the ball, allowing the batter to potentially reach first base since there were no runners on and fewer than two outs. However, the Sunfish hitter abandoned his attempt and returned to the dugout, resulting in an out. The Sunfish manager argued that the hitter fouled the ball off, but I knew this wasn't correct. He insisted I seek assistance, but I had the final say. Tristyn clarified that the ball struck the hitter as he swung, rendering him out and the play dead—thus, the runner who advanced to third was not sent back to second, which was our only error in judgment.

Later in the game, a Sunfish runner attempted to steal home from third base. The pitcher stepped off the mound and threw home, successfully tagging out the runner. The Sunfish manager vehemently claimed a balk had occurred, but upon reviewing the video later at the hotel, we confirmed the pitcher's move was legal. Besides these incidents and some notable scoring, the game overall was decent.

June 12

The Sioux Falls Sunfish are hosting the Souris Valley Sabre Dogs in this three-game series, and it started with last night's smooth game and win for the Fish. I'll feel good if I can have a plate game like that tonight. I think I'm more likely to have those kinds of games with Tristyn because he seems more encouraging and likes to help me with the little details of my craft. He says I've got all the big stuff down (Thanks, umpire school), so there's just little stuff that can make things smoother.

I think the biggest thing he wants me to do is loosen up and have some fun. That's easier on the bases than at the plate, but I'm going to try to feel good tonight. It's like I tell athletes: If you go into it trying to have fun, you'll be more likely to win, and you'll look up, realize you're winning, and realize that the game is going by fast. However, if you go into a game pressing to win, thinking that fun is a byproduct, not the goal, you'll be more likely to put unnecessary pressure on yourself, making you fail. Dang, I'm good.

June 13

Just because you have your third ejection of the season doesn't mean the game was bad. In fact, other than that and the high scoring, it was quite good. Tristyn has been working with me on my plate stance and trying to get me more into the slot (The space between the batter and catcher). I tried that, and I felt good.

The ejection was the Sunfish manager Walker Bullington being picky about how I went about giving his catcher extra time after being hit by a foul ball. I asked if he was alright, took some steps back, and then went and brushed off the plate, something that umpires customarily do to give the catcher time to recuperate. However, Bullington was yelling aggressively and adamantly that I should go out to the mound and "figure it out!" By then, the catcher was fine, and it was time to keep the game rolling, so I firmly told him, "That's enough," but to no avail. He continued as if I hadn't said anything (Tristyn told me the manager said, "I'm not done yet"), which was an easy toss. Somehow, he couldn't believe it, but if you don't show me up on the field, you don't have to face consequences like that. Sorry, not sorry.

Today I have the bases, then two days off before going back to Pierre, so that will be a nice break.

June 14

Today is the first of two off days for Tristyn and me, so we stayed up late, slept late, and went out for a relaxing lunch with some dessert. Good day. After that, we went to Walmart to pick up a few things, and that was it.

We go back to Pierre on Wednesday when I have a plate game. My first plate game with Tristyn was there, and they'll be playing the same visiting team, so hopefully, I can just replicate that first plate job on Wednesday.

June 17

I know it's been a couple of days since I last posted, but I've just been trying to enjoy my off days, one of which (Monday) we spent that evening at the Sunfish ballpark watching a game with another umpire crew working that game because the schedule is crazy. The length of that game was about the same as that of my plate job here in Pierre last night, which was just under three and a half hours. I did well last night, but there was a good bit of scoring, which makes games go longer. There was a low and inside pitch that just caught the plate that I called a strike three on, and I felt bad doing it because it was such a good pitch, and it would've been hard to hit, but hey, a strike is a strike.

I'll have the bases, the Sioux Falls Sunfish, and the Pierre Trappers again tonight. In fact, I don't think I'll have a single game with Tristyn that doesn't involve the Sunfish for at least a week or two.

If you were to ask me if I prefer to call games behind the plate or on the bases, I would probably say the bases, but I don't think it's that clear-cut. It's easier to get into a routine in the game behind the plate, and you feel good after finishing it up, particularly if it was a good game, but the bases are more relaxing, at least when there's no one on base. I like being on the bases after a plate job, especially in a doubleheader, because I feel so free without all the equipment, and I feel like I can fight anyone who comes out to argue with me. That's a little ironic, considering that you would think that the protection would provide more confidence in that regard, but I guess it's because I have more of a range of motion, and I can run better on the bases.

We'll have a doubleheader on Sunday (Father's Day) in Carol, Iowa, because an American Legion team is using the Sunfish Ballpark this weekend. The Expedition League is considering expanding to Carol (though some people in this league say it can't handle the teams it's got, which I agree with), so we'll have those games there. It should be interesting.

June 20

There has been a big cluster of stuff the past couple of days:

If you remember, the league put two twenty-year-olds in the same crew, as if that was a good idea. Eventually, they did switch the crews, but before that, the schedule that I'm on now was changed for this weekend from Grand Forks, ND, to Sioux Falls. However, just a couple of days ago, they changed that from Sioux Falls to Carroll, Iowa, because the college team wasn't given full use of the field. Some other league has priority over this one, so they had to move this series. But here in Carroll, the league booked all the hotel rooms for both teams, and the umpires an hour and a half away. The players don't have it as bad because they don't drive, but we do. When my partner tried to get a room at a closer hotel and told the league that they could cancel our room at the hotel far away, they couldn't do it, mainly because the staff there can't speak English, as evidenced by how my partner tried to contact them earlier today. So the league isn't reimbursing my partner for this room on his backup credit card because he lost his main one.

I almost forgot: We had a game last evening, and I had the plate. No problem there, other than all the ones I've already mentioned. Today, a doubleheader. I'm okay with that, too, because the games will be seven innings, and I'm used to those from high school season. But the league seriously expected us to drive an hour and a half to and from the ballpark after two games, then get up the next day and drive seven hours to Grand Forks in Iowa.

So yeah, it was a lot to deal with, and this league is pretty shaky right now, but at least Merchants Park here in Carroll is nice.

That base game in Pierre was pretty good. Early on, there were some issues with balks, including one we called, but that's what we (umpires) were there to do. The field in Pierre is dusty, so after plate jobs, my shoes and the bottoms of my pants are all dirty. We have cleaning agents for that, though, with Scrubbing Bubbles being the go-to for shoe needs. It would probably be better if they just watered the field, but I'll take getting dirty if it means a quick and smooth game.

After two travel days to get here, with a night spent in Sioux Falls to help with splitting up the drive, we got to Carroll, figured out our hotel cluster, and then had a game that evening with me behind the plate. Except for a lengthy first inning and some late scoring, the game flew by, and I was proud of that. My strike zone probably wasn't the best it could've been, which was unfortunate because I wanted to have a good game in that ballpark, but my zone was still good. It's hard to call the low/inside strike for some reason. Everyone seems to want the pitch at or around the letters, but I don't always give that. I always go for below the letters, though starting in the seventh last night, I started calling it and didn't hear anything about it. Both starting pitchers were showing bad body language, and while nothing got to the point of warnings or ejections, I'm not afraid to be firm with these guys if I need to be because if they try to be disrespectful back, they'll have an early shower. I also missed some rotations in certain situations once the ball was hit, but that was just a one-time thing that is usually no problem.

Tonight, I'll have the bases for the first seven-inning game of the doubleheader, then my first-ever plate game on a consecutive day, also seven innings. I'm looking forward to seeing this nice ballpark from the view on the bases.

June 21

I'm writing this from Grand Forks, North Dakota, just an hour north of Fargo, home to Roger Maris and his museum and grave, both of which Tristyn and I plan to visit tomorrow. We have today and tomorrow off, with today being our travel day.

Yesterday, we finished a three-game series between the Wheat City Whiskey Jacks, who usually play in Canada but are currently in Grand Forks due to virus concerns, and the Sioux Falls Sunfish in Carroll, Iowa. My first game on the bases was a high-scoring affair. The Jacks' manager argued that the Sunfish shortstop didn't touch the base on a double play, which I found ridiculous since it looked clear to me that he did. When he continued to yell at me as he returned to the third base coach's box, I sternly told him that was enough. After the previous night's dispute about a batter's position during a home run, which I later confirmed was baseless, I find it hard to take the Jacks' manager seriously. I've heard their team has a reputation for being sore winners and losers, which I experienced firsthand during my plate game.

At the bottom of the third, they kept complaining about my strike zone, so I removed my mask and made it clear to everyone on their side that further comments about balls and strikes would result in ejections. The silence from their side until the last inning was telling.

I could've ejected at least three players last night instead of just one. Recently, something clicked in my brain, and I've stopped caring about being nice when the time for that has passed. I let some things slide even after issuing a warning, which I now regret. Ejecting more players would send a clear message (and the league imposes suspensions for ejections). If I do that enough, the problems should diminish. If issues do arise, they'll be easier to resolve because the players will understand the consequences. Ultimately, I need to enforce the rules firmly and consistently to maintain control and ensure smooth games.

June 25

We went an hour south of Grand Forks to Fargo, the hometown of Roger Maris. In Fargo, there are two Maris-related attractions: the Roger Maris Museum, located in a mall, and his grave, which is in a cemetery near the airport. The museum is a long wall encased in glass with lots of mementos and memorabilia from Maris' career. It shows off jerseys, pictures, equipment, and many awards Maris earned during his career, although two items—a belt and the 1960 AL MVP award—were stolen in July 2016 and have not yet been recovered. There's also a doorway leading into a small theater with original Yankee Stadium seats from Maris' playing days, pictures on the walls, and a screen showing a documentary about Maris. It is incredibly fascinating and a must-see for any baseball or history buff. The simplicity of the museum (a wall and a small theater) and Maris' humility are exemplified through the exhibit's content. In the documentary, Mickey Mantle is quoted by Bob Costas as saying, when Maris died, "There's no justice in this," implying that Mantle felt he deserved to die early, not Maris.

After Tristyn and I finished up at the museum, we headed to the cemetery where Maris is buried. We eventually found his grave and took some pictures of the large diamond-shaped headstone. There were baseballs and cards placed by it in tribute. Seeing all this about Roger Maris, especially after watching the movie 61, was interesting—it's a great baseball movie, and it's on YouTube for free if you're okay with Spanish subtitles.

Later in the day, we watched the Fargo-Moorhead RedHawks American Association (independent league) play against the Chicago Dogs. All three umpires were guys Tristyn knows, and Dustin, one of the umpires, got us the tickets. We had seats right behind home plate, next to the runway behind home, where the umpires and promotional staff enter and exit. In the first inning, the two-hole hitter for the Dogs came up, and I instantly recognized the name—Anfernee Grier. He attended my high school until the coaches told him he wasn't good enough, so he transferred to Russell County High, where he got drafted by the Detroit Tigers but ended up playing for the Auburn Tigers. He was drafted by the D-backs in 2016 and was cut in 2020 when the minor leagues were reorganized. He eventually signed with the Chicago Dogs. I got his attention between innings, and he promised me an autograph after the game. I said, "War Eagle," and he smiled. After the game, a bullpen pitcher got him for me, and I got to talk to him about what brings us so far from home (he asked me first). I told him I was an umpire in a college league, and he signed a ticket and a baseball for me. He went 5-5 with a home run, so hopefully, he won't be here much longer. It was a stand-up move for him to keep his promise. Hopefully, I'll see him again soon.

The day after all this, I had the bases for a high-scoring game. Tristyn said he never really settled into the game, but we got through it.

The next day was a doubleheader. I had the plate first and had to make a batter's interference call during a stolen base attempt. I had never called it before, so I was visibly thrown off, which an umpire never wants to show. At first, I didn't call it because I felt there wasn't quite interference, but the Moo assistant coach came to speak with me, and I decided it was interference. Then I had to enforce it, which I asked Tristyn about to make sure. Robby, the Whiskey Jacks manager, wasn't happy, saying, "If you don't know the rules, you don't need to be out there." He's right—I should have handled this smoother, but it didn't happen. Now I know. Another heckle from the Jacks' dugout about me looking young ("You should be more focused on getting your driver's license") needed to be shut down, though I openly admitted it was funny. I don't like to be unlikeable or too uptight, particularly with teams that like to have fun. It was also smooth sailing, especially since I've been improving my plate stance, head height, and strike zone, which is how tonight's game in Sioux Falls between the Hastings Sodbusters and the Sunfish went.

In the base game following the plate game in Grand Forks, the Jacks played Zoe Hicks, the only girl in the Expedition League. Tristyn told me after the game that the Moo catcher asked him, "You're gonna walk her because she's a girl?" Tristyn replied, "No, I'm gonna walk her because your pitcher can't throw strikes." She hit a ground ball during one of her at-bats and was thrown out at first. I had to adjust my standard "He's out" call to just "Out." Our training emphasizes good timing, so the slight delay wasn't so bad.

Overall, it's been an eventful stretch. Working with Tristyn has proven beneficial for my development as an umpire, providing constructive feedback and a supportive environment. Handling disputes, making crucial calls, and maintaining a sense of humor will serve me well as I refine my skills. These experiences are shaping me into a resilient and adaptable umpire.

June 27

Last night, I got hit by a line drive on the foot for the second time this week, and it still hurts today. If it's not better after tonight's game and by tomorrow morning, I'll probably have it looked at by either the trainer or the Sunfish's general manager's wife, who is a foot specialist.

Honestly, I wouldn't mind if there were an issue because it might mean I would get sent home—a place I've wanted to go since the first game of the season in Caldwell, Idaho. I've seen some cool stuff up here and learned a lot, but I'm just not feeling it anymore. I haven't been since I was in Casper, Wyoming. It would be dishonest and unhealthy to act like everything is great when it isn't.

June 29

Yesterday was supposed to be an off day, but Mitch from the league asked us to work a game in Fremont, Nebraska, home of the Moo. We were out late in Fremont, two hours away from Sioux Falls. I think George Tyree and Anthony Atkinson, the crew that was in Fremont, weren't feeling well, so Mitch asked us to cover that game since we were the closest crew. It was a good game—I had the bases, and nothing strange happened except fireworks going off somewhere.

Tonight's game behind the plate was also good. Tristyn said it was one of the best plate games he'd seen me have. A play at the plate scored the tying run, and my gut said safe, though there's a chance the Sunfish catcher tagged the runner on his back. No one stirred up a fuss. Similarly, a simple judgment call that Tristyn probably missed initially went smoothly. I'll have the bases tomorrow so I can avoid the same mistakes he made.

July 1

Thank goodness it's July. I just wish it was August. Last night's game on the bases wasn't bad. There was a possible foul off the foot that we didn't catch, and I may have missed a pickoff, but it was smooth other than a twelve-run eighth inning. I'll have the plate tonight, and I'm coming off a nice plate game in Sioux Falls, so I'll strive for a repeat of that before tomorrow's off day.

However, the base game did not take place in Sioux Falls; it was back in Fremont for the second time this week. George and Anthony were having issues with both teams and received several complaints, so the league decided to switch us and them to the other city. I won't be surprised to see those two get sent home soon.

Connor, the guy Tristyn was working with before me, has been promoted. Chad has gone home for a family issue. Mitch removed Jake, my former crew partner, from the GroupMe, so he's probably going home. And now these two may be going home soon. I've heard that the league was going to send one more person home, which may have been Jake, but I have no idea. They're having trouble replacing guys. Before yesterday, I thought I would be sent home soon, but within 36 hours, that thought has diminished significantly. Even if the league still wants to send me home, they may not be able to because they can't find enough umpires to come up here. Time will tell.

Hopefully, this month will turn to August quickly. Depending on whether we have to call the All-Star Game, July may not go by so quickly. And if we get postseason assignments, I'll probably have to stay here for another week. We don't have too many more off days, and Tristyn says that helps time go by quicker, so I guess I'll see how that goes.

July 4

This day's blog entry was made in video form. The internet link: *https://youtu.be/W_I5ZCLUNJE*

July 8

I apologize for not writing every day. I'm getting tired more easily with all the travel and poor internet connections. However, I have been calling games regularly. This includes the plate game on Sunday, which I mentioned in my video post, a base game in Dickinson, ND, where I had my first ejection on the bases (Big Sticks manager Billy Tomblin), and a plate game last night, which went pretty well.

In the base game in Dickinson, a Sabre Dogs runner was attempting to advance from second to third base on a pitch that the catcher bobbled slightly. The catcher recovered quickly enough to throw to third ahead of the runner. However, the runner managed to slide around the awaiting tag. Remember, just because the ball beats the runner doesn't mean an out on a tag play—only on force plays. Since the runner was safe, that's what I signaled.

Billy Tomblin rushed towards me without asking for time. While we could have penalized him for this, we didn't. I'll give him credit—his first words were, "Tell me what you saw." The conversation got caught up in his question, "Where was he tagged?" I responded that it didn't matter since the runner was safe. After a brief exchange, he walked back toward the dugout. However, he turned around and continued to argue. A few words are one thing, but continuous arguing is another. So, I turned my body to the left and threw my finger up, signaling his ejection.

My mistake was letting Billy come all the way back to me. I probably should have met him halfway so it would take less time for him to leave after our discussion. Nothing new came about during the continued delay, but Tristyn came around soon enough to lead him off the field.

Initially, Tristyn and I thought the ejection didn't necessarily have to happen, but our league supervisor thought it was good. After thinking about it more (albeit at the bar), Tristyn also agreed. So, I feel good about the decision.

July 9

Last night, we visited Minot, ND, for Tristyn's only game there this season, and my third, but our last regardless, as we're headed back to South Dakota's capital city once again.

So, how was last night's game on the bases for me? Alex, the Sabre Dogs manager, came out to me once and was worked up over a couple of calls at first base, but I only missed one of the others I had. He said he would show me the video tomorrow because I don't think he knew that another crew would be in town for their games this weekend. Haha.

During the sixth inning, there was some close lightning, so we stopped the game after Tristyn rang up a guy on strike one. It didn't take long after that for the rain to start coming down, and for the league president, who was there, to call the game. You know it's bad rain when on a turf field. They can play the game that quickly. That's the first suspended called game I've ever had, and surprisingly, Tristyn's too.

July 11

I've had two plate and base games within the past two days. The first plate game was a solid, regular nine-inning match. The base game was the first of a long doubleheader yesterday. The next plate game went into the eighth inning, which is an extra inning for seven-inning doubleheader games. It was not too bad overall, but I had a rough night.

During the game, I got hit in the thigh and hand by a pitch, and later, a foul ball knocked my mask clean off, giving me a headache for the rest of the night. You can imagine how I felt when the game went to extras and there was a complicated play involving two rundowns and a runner passing another at third base. Tristyn initially called one runner out for being tagged, but we later declared two outs because the runner who was passed was also out. However, that isn't correct. It's the runner who passes another who is out, so we should've only called one out. Shoot.

I'll have the bases tonight before we head to Dickinson tomorrow. The All-Star break starts next Monday, giving us a week before then and two weeks of the season after that unless I get picked for the postseason. Given my experience, I think I might not get picked, but we'll see. I'm hoping I don't because I've seen enough out here.

I'm looking forward to seeing everyone back home once again.

July 13

The base game in Pierre on Sunday passed quickly when scoring wasn't occurring, as is typical. We return to Pierre tomorrow for two more games before moving on. Tristyn and I enjoy Pierre; the general manager is great, meals are always home-cooked, the ballpark is nice (though the dirt is quite dusty), and the capitol building is conveniently close. Here in Dickinson, everything seems positive as well. The hotel is excellent, the team draws a decent crowd, and the meals are good.

Last night's plate game here in Dickinson was likely the best I've ever had. Tristyn seemed to think so, too. Aside from one diving catch where I had a moment's trouble seeing but corrected myself for the right call, everything else was nearly perfect. I rotated well as needed (even handling a play at third base), projected my calls clearly, had a consistent strike zone and felt sharp overall. I was settled and confident from the first pitch, which hasn't happened all season.

My secret that day: I made myself angry before the game. I've found that I'm more confident when I'm a bit angry; it makes me feel like nobody will question my calls. I wasn't rude to anyone on the field, but I carried myself as if I didn't care what others thought or did. This mindset prepared me for any situation. Thankfully, I didn't need to issue warnings or eject anyone, so that anger wasn't necessary. The two times managers questioned me (once about potential batter's interference and once about an inside pitch I called a ball), I calmly explained my call, and that was the end. Perhaps they sensed my confidence, realizing that any challenge could disrupt the game, which worked in my favor.

During the game, I noticed details I usually miss (like where the batter was in the box and a couple of foul balls off the knob of the bat, which I've struggled with before). I felt sure about every call, even the borderline ones. The game ended 9-4 and lasted two hours and twenty minutes, a testament to how smoothly it ran. I maintained my confident demeanor from the moment I stepped onto the field until I left the umpire's room after the game.

In the later innings, there was a 3-2 pitch that I called a ball, allowing the Whiskey Jacks batter to take a base. Afterward, the

Big Sticks decided to change pitchers. The Big Sticks manager, Billy approached me with his lineup card to inform me of his substitutions. Before he did, he asked where I thought the last pitch missed. Any coaches reading this, that's how you handle it: no drama, just straightforward communication.

July 15

The base game in Dickinson went as well as my plate game did, at least for me, and I kept the same stern mindset in it, as well as last night's plate game in Pierre, which would be my last here. I did well, but the game went twelve innings, and I was a little all over the place with my strike zone at the time. Oh well, it happens. I heard stuff from hitters and catchers, but I'm not afraid to eject, so I have the last word, even if only on the field. If someone wants to complain to the league, that's a whole different regard, and it's out of my control. I can control things on the field, and that's what I'm being paid to do, so I will continue to do that for the rest of this season, which is only about three weeks, not counting the postseason. The All-Star Game is next week in Casper, Wyoming, and the crew for that game still has not been announced, even though we were told it would be disclosed on Monday. On our way there, Tristyn and I plan to at least drive by Mount Rushmore. If not, stop and check it out, depending on whether there's more to do there other than that and Crazy Horse. That will be a long drive from Grand Forks (where we'll be before the break) to Casper, but oh well again. The break will be well-appreciated.

July 16

No. That simple, two-letter word—the shortest multi-letter word in the English language—holds a lot of meaning for me right now. It signifies "No, I still have three weeks out here," or "No, a six-hour drive to Grand Forks today," or None, as in how many hits the Whiskey Jacks had yesterday.

Yes, that's right. Yesterday in Pierre, the Trappers pitcher threw a complete game no-hitter, marking the first in Trappers history and the second against the Whiskey Jacks this season (the previous one was exactly a month earlier on June 15th). The final pitch may have been a little outside, but Tristyn called it, emphasizing the hitter's need to protect with two strikes.

However, my main takeaway from that game involves a balk situation. I didn't call one when I possibly should have. I mentioned it to Tristyn between innings, and he said it was nothing, so I let it go. We'll review the video when we get to Grand Forks.

Tonight, I'm behind the plate for the first of three games between the Whiskey Jacks and the Trappers, the final three games before the All-Star break. I've been performing well behind the plate, aiming for more smooth games. If an ejection is necessary, I'm prepared—I feel like I'm due for one anyway. I currently have five, which I think ties me for first. Time is still passing, sometimes quicker than others. I'm eagerly anticipating boarding the plane to Atlanta, knowing this chapter is finally ending. It's a refreshing thought, especially knowing I'll soon be reunited with my family and friends.

July 18

The plate game on Friday wasn't bad, but the Whiskey Jacks catcher was talking all night. It wasn't anything terrible, just a lot of "Both ways" and "That's there" and other firm comments. Then he didn't like those calls when he was at bat. Not my problem.

Yesterday's game with the Trappers was another story. They had a runner called out for leaving early from third base on a tag-up, gave up eight runs in the first inning, and seemed to have every close call go against them, though not intentionally. But a couple of plays at third base that they really didn't agree with led to me ejecting a player after each incident. Those were my first two player ejections, and I believe I now lead the league with seven. I didn't eject them just to retake the lead—they had crossed the line. One called me blind and the other used expletives continuously when leaving the field. Interestingly, their second baseman had been chatting with me between innings, saying he thought I'd make a good umpire one day but needed to be stricter. He even mentioned wanting to see me eject someone before the season ended. Well...

He wasn't one of the ejections, by the way. But his whole team wasn't thrilled with me during that game, right up to the last pitch when Tristyn asked if a Trappers hitter went around on a check-swing, and I said he did. They were furious, but later at the hotel, I went down to where Tristyn was to review my reports before sending them. Many of the players were there, and everything was calm. That's the thing about this league (and sports in general)—between the lines, things can get heated, but off the field, we all know it's entertainment, and we all want to go home.

The All-Star break starts tomorrow, and everyone is ready for it. If only the season ended today. We're still pushing through, but we'll see how it goes.

July 20

The last game before the All-Star break was pretty good as it was under three hours; not too much complaining, the players had a lot of fun, and a feeling of relief afterward that we had some time off, albeit that we had to spend yesterday driving from Grand Forks ND to Casper WY, a very long drive. We did get here in time for the Home Run Derby, which someone from the Western Nebraska Pioneers won. I won't have the Pioneers this season, but this is my 2nd time being in Casper. I won't have the All-Star Game, so it will be nice to watch a game here. The ASG crew consists of three guys, including Tristyn, who I went to umpire school with. I don't know the four-umpire system, so I couldn't work the ASG, and maybe that means I can't work the postseason either, although one guy who probably can already bought his plane ticket for August 8th, the day after the season. Hopefully, it's refundable.

When we got to Mike Lansing Field yesterday, Tristyn, George Tyree, and Anthony Atkinson went and got beers, as the latter two said they would for Tristyn and I after we covered one of their games in Fremont and later swapped cities with them a few weeks back. As I stood watching stuff on the field, I feel a nudge behind me. It was Tristyn with a Michelob-Ultra in his hand, giving it to me. Of course, I declined, but it didn't go to waste as he drank it after finishing his first one.

I hope to get enough rest here in Casper to have a really

good plate game on Thursday in Butte's 3 Legends Field, where the Mining City Tommyknockers will host the Pierre Trappers for four games.

July 21

Ok, so today was a real crapshoot, but cool too. Let's start with the drive itself. It was an all-day drive from Casper, WY to Butte, MT, with some slow-moving traffic along the way and no cell service in other parts.

Tristyn's car GPS stuff acts up sometimes. We finally get to Butte, and the hotel we're staying at says they have us coming in tomorrow. However, our check-out day from Casper was today, so I guess the league and the teams thought we wouldn't sleep tonight because we weren't the only crew with that issue. That hotel called their manager, and they got us settled in this week-old hotel, so it's really nice. Now it's nearly 2 am back home.

But it wasn't all bad. This was the day after the All-Star Game, which was fun to be at because food was free for umpires, I got to see a game in this league without having to stress about calls on the field, and I got to catch up with some umpire school buddies.

Today, we drove through Grand Teton National Park and Yellowstone National Park, where we saw Old Faithful erupt and heard some girl behind us make lame jokes about the geyser. I picked up two postcards and an ornament at a shop there. I will also be mailing a baseball to my Pop in Huntsville from Independence Day. On Father's Day, in addition to wearing light blue mask pads, I kept a ball from my plate game that day and sent it home to my dad with a note about the game. I will do the same for my Pop when I get to a post office or UPS/FedEx store.

July 23

Yesterday I had the plate in Butte, Montana, where the Mining City Tommyknockers hosted the Pierre Trappers for the 1st of 4 games here. I started out feeling uncomfortable, which tends to happen when I'm at a place I haven't been to before, but I settled in when I started telling myself to "Watch the white thing." That kept me from thinking too much. A fan on the Trappers side was messing with them in the late innings, so we had to settle that down. I don't care for fans anymore, anyway. If I had been calling games last season when no one was at the games, that would've been great because fans are pretty well clueless, especially when they're rooting for a particular team, because any call that goes against that team they think is wrong. "Well, that's just how fans are, you know." Oh yeah, fans being the most clueless people in the world is "just how it is" now? Once again, this is an example of how America has normalized ignorance.

I'll have the bases tonight, so I won't be able to see the view from home plate like I did last night, which consists of the city on the left, and mountains on the right, one of which having "Our Lady of the Rockies," a big statue of Mary.

July 24

I just got done with a fun base game, from a good smell at one point to a tie at first base that I called the guy out on (because tie does NOT go to the runner, if you know how the rulebook words it), and a successful hidden ball trick. The Trapper's first baseman passed me after a base hit and said he was going to keep the ball, and as he passed his pitcher, he pretended to give the pitcher the ball but didn't. After that, we all got in position, except for the pitcher, who couldn't step on the rubber without the ball. I made sure the pitcher didn't toe the rubber. I saw the tag applied to the runner as he stepped off the base, saw the ball once again, and called the runner out. The runner and the first base coach had that look of embarrassment in their eyes, and I even told the runner I was sorry, but I had to do it, and he knew he simply was the victim of the hidden ball trick. There wasn't much opposition from the Tommyknockers side except for a coach coming out for clarification. I jogged over to him to attempt to calm the situation before it even got lit up. I told him right away that the pitcher is allowed to be on the dirt of the mound without the ball, as long as he doesn't feint a move associated with his pitching delivery, but not on the rubber. He said ok and moved on.

July 25

The plate game was pretty good when it finally got started after the Tommyknockers ran out of chalk for the foul lines, so they had to take a little longer to finish them. Other than that, people will always disagree with some pitches and let you hear about it, particularly late in the game, but I felt pretty good. At the end of the game, both teams started going at each other, so we stuck around for a couple of moments longer to diffuse that. But there were no ejections.

That is, until today's base game. It started with the Tommyknockers not having enough baseballs, so we delayed the game a little bit again to see which baseballs out of the rag-tag ones we had available from each team's batting practice stash we could use. Still, we figured the game would eventually end because the baseballs would run out, and the Tommyknockers would have to forfeit. Unfortunately, that did not happen. What happened, however, was two more ejections for Tristyn and me, joining the ejection club with two of his own. Mine were the Tommyknocker's assistant coach and a player after a check-swing call—the coach essentially questioned by ability, which is a no-go. I then was very firm with him about how he could not disrespect me simply because I looked young. The hitter yelled something a pitch later, so I tossed him, too. He said after the game that he was talking about a balk, buuut...don't tie your shoes in a watermelon batch, buddy (Shout out to those of you who know what that means).

If you go back and watch the video of the first ejection, it may look like I went after the Tommyknockers coach when I was firm with him, but I don't care how I look. I'm trying to get through this season, and no one will stand in my way. I already know that umpiring isn't something I want to dedicate my life to, especially after this season. If you read the posts during umpire school, you may remember something I put in one of those posts that is one of the reasons I don't want to call baseball games as a career: it's just another endeavor in life that requires one to sacrifice their individual identity for the sake of a group, cause, or occupation. I used a George Carlin quote to oversimplify it: "If it requires a uniform, it's a worthless endeavor." So, when I finish this season, it'll be back to the drawing board for me, which will be okay because I hadn't even thought about umpiring very long anyway, so it's not like it was ever a lifelong "dream." But now is the time to experiment for me-when I'm young.

Tristyn's two ejections came after the first out at the bottom of the 9th inning after the Trappers pitcher struck out a Tommyknocker hitter, and they both started chirping at each other. The benches began to leak, things started to settle a bit, and then the pitcher decided to keep going, after which Tristyn tossed him and the Tommyknocker hitter. His report will be more straightforward than my two.

Somehow, we got through that game with one baseball to spare, albeit nearly four hours. None of the games in this four-game series were quick games. All of them being over three hours. Now we have to leave at 6:30 tomorrow morning and follow the Tommyknockers to Dickinson, ND, where they will play the Badlands Big Sticks for four games. Both teams are vying for the second postseason spot in their division since it looks like the Souris Valley Sabre Dogs will win that division again in the second half of the season, so the second-place team will go to the postseason if that happens.

July 27

Yesterday, after we left a couple hours later than we wanted, we got into Dickinson, ND in pretty good time. The drive from Butte to here is all interstate. I nearly fell asleep several times during the car ride, and I was tired last night, especially after a plate game. I was also so exhausted after the game in Butte, where we had four ejections that I missed an entire conversation in our umpire group message where a guy asked me who I threw out. Tristyn did my talking for me, but the best part about the whole exchange between everyone there was when Garrett Forsythe, a guy I went to umpire school with, said to me, "Sam, you have the biggest dick on the field I've ever seen." This was a reference to Junior telling us that we should have that mentality when we walk onto the field. What's also funny is that this happened at three in the morning, so apparently, a bunch of the umpires were still awake at that hour except me.

That game wasn't all that bad, except for some minor stuff. On a check swing, I point at the hitter and say we went around. Tristyn thought I was pointing towards him, asking, and he signaled no. This happened a few games ago, but no big deal was made. This time, the Big Sticks manager came out and tried to tell me I was pointing toward Tristyn, and then I signaled yes. I know what I was pointing at, so how can he supposedly tell me what I was pointing towards that confidently? I'm not sure. Tristyn told me later that I took a little long to make the "yes he did" call, so if I have to think about it like that, just go to him next time. Fair enough. It was a little thing that was made a bigger thing by a manager being overzealous. I want to stay at nine ejections for the season, but at this rate, I have no idea if that will stick.

Tristyn said I got a little tight with my zone in the last inning, which I didn't even notice. There were some low pitches that I guess I was probably calling strikes that I was letting go, but it's not like those are obvious one way or the other. Wouldn't life be so much better if everyone just took a breath, relaxed, and didn't make such a big deal out of everything? I know the Tommyknockers know this because, in one of the early innings, there was a play on the field (I think like a pickoff attempt for something small like that), their dugout made a joke towards Tristyn (not hostile), and he smiled. The dugout noticed, and someone said, "See, baseball's fun." Yeah, it should be. Why don't we make it that way?

The Big Sticks do have an artificial infield (which I do better on, except Pierre sometimes, but we don't go back there again this season), so there is no need for chalk and, therefore, no chance of running out of it. They also have plenty of baseballs. This organization is run very well. There are decent crowds, fan/community involvement, smooth on-field promotions, postgame meals cooked by host families, etc. A big reason is that they have an excellent general manager, who is also an umpire, so he gets what we need and do.

I have five plate games left and eleven total, with the season ending on August 7. I won't be on a postseason crew, so that means on August 8, my mother's birthday, I'll get to fly home, likely from Bismark, ND, not too far from here in Dickinson, which is where we end the season when the Big Sticks play the Canyon County Spuds for two games. Do you recognize that team name? That's the team I started the season with at their place in Caldwell, ID, so they'll come full circle to begin and end my season. Oh boy, I'm looking forward to that.

July 28

Yesterday's base game went pretty well, with it being under three hours (more accurately, 2:20). It was pretty smooth, and that's how I like to think today's plate game went. Other than an extra inning, me getting hit on the hand by a foul ball, and me reaching double digits in ejections (A pretty simple ejection: dugout running their mouths, I warn them, the guy keeps on, gone. He said after the game that he told Tristyn he was trying to get ejected anyway because he leaves for home tomorrow). It still was a good game, and it was 2:45, perfect for extra innings. Some female fan tried to yell at me that I was not old enough to be on the field. Well, she doesn't have...ehh, let me not get canceled. Someone else also told me to go home a couple of times. I wish I could. I had a fairly expansive strike zone and kept it that way the whole game, so there isn't much rational complaining that can be done. I'll have the bases before returning to Butte for three games with these two teams tomorrow. After a three-game series in Butte with the Tommyknockers taking on the Casper Horseheads, and a two-game series in Dickinson where the Big Sticks will take on the Canyon County Spuds. I'm ready to get finished. Hurry up.

My dad told me to look out for an email tomorrow confirming the purchase of plane tickets for the 8th for a flight from Bismarck, ND, to Atlanta, GA, with a 2:41 layover in Minneapolis-plenty of time to contemplate what the heck I just did with two and a half months of my life.

There are nine more games left, four being plate games. The schedule is passing, but if only it could pass a little quicker. Getting back home to familiarity and where things make sense will feel great. I can't tell yet if walking back into my house will feel like a new experience that brings me joy or if it will indeed feel like I'm back where I belong. Either way, I'm champing at the bit. Yes, "champing" is correct, not "chomping" to get there and find out. I'll see ya'll there.

July 29

It wasn't a bad base game tonight, consisting of two grand slams, at least one other home run, and a few interesting calls. I believe the first interesting call came in the fourth inning. Big Sticks hitter grounds to shortstop and tosses to second base for the out, but the second baseman loses the ball on the transfer. But I read it as a loose ball, and the runner is safe. Tommyknockers manager comes out for clarification. I correct myself, saying that the runner is out. Big Sticks manager comes out wondering...pretty much what the heck. We got the call right, but a sticky situation transpired along the way. I saw the ball come out and automatically read that as the runner being safe. If I had a little more time (you don't have much time on potential double plays to read the play at second base because you have to turn your attention to first base quickly), I may have been able to read it correctly as the ball coming out on the transfer, but...tomorrow is a new day. More accurately, it's the first of six games we have in Butte, and the first of three games these same two teams play there. They're tied for their division's second postseason spot, so someone will lead after that series. The Spuds are also crawling their way up in the standings, so the last two games we have in Dickinson might be interesting.

The second interesting call came later on a line drive to the Tommyknockers shortstop, who threw to first to get the Big Sticks runner out. I called it safe because my angle at that play wasn't very good. In the two-umpire system, I'm between the mound and second base, just on the first base side, and my angle is looking at the back of the runner. The Tommyknockers manager asked me to ask Tristyn about it because he had a better view, which I realized. He has the runner out, so we also got that call right.

In an inning between those calls, I called the Tommyknockers runner safe at second on a ground ball because the Big Sticks' shortstop was off the base, and it was another right call.

July 3

Yesterday, we got into Butte. I was worn out from the road, much like the teams were, but I called a nice plate game. The Tommyknockers' starting pitcher was working incredibly quickly and efficiently, so I thought I would have an under two-hour game until the sixth inning or so when some more runs began scoring. I've told all of you before that if a plate umpire has a sub-two-hour game, his partner/crew buys a steak dinner. We will have one on Monday evening when we have off anyway, but I felt good about that game, except for the headache I got in the first inning when I got clocked in the mask with a foul ball. That got me good.

I have the bases tonight, and these two teams are batting for the last postseason spot in their division. It doesn't matter to me who wins, but Tristyn secretly wants the Big Sticks to win because it's a shorter drive to Souris Valley, who's already clinched, than from here (Butte) to there. Plus, the Big Sticks have better all-around operations.

This time next week, I'll be getting dressed and preparing for the final game this season. So close, yet so far.

August 2

You may want to grab a drink and sip awhile for everything I'm about to tell you. I know I've said this a couple other times this season, but the past couple of days have been so crazy. This isn't just a schedule change or ejection. So, Saturday night in Butte, the Badlands Big Sticks, and the hometown Mining City Tommyknockers are battling for the last postseason spot, which starts the following Monday. I'll be home at that point. Anyway, in the game's middle innings, there's a rundown in which the Big

Sticks manager says the runner was out of the basepath, and I said he wasn't. Later in the game, the Tommyknockers bring a pitcher in who isn't on the lineup card, but he doesn't have to be eligible. My partner tells the Big Sticks manager this, but he doesn't like it. We go on until the next half-inning when he comes out and says he wants to protest the game over it. We have the rule right, and protests aren't even allowed anymore, so we held up the game for ten minutes to find the rule in the book, returned, and resumed the game that the Big Sticks won anyway. I don't know why he protested that, but instead of my out-of-baseline thing, I don't know because he might've had more success there. Other than that, again, protests aren't allowed.

Also, during that game, the Zooperstars were in town here, so the first thing I started thinking about was, "I guess I'm gonna get hit again," since the last two times I've been calling a game on the bases that they were here for, I've gotten hit by a ball. Mitch, the league VP, was in town driving them in a small cart from their changing area to the field. As an inning was about to start and Mitch was driving back, he said to the Tommyknocker first baseman (I think his name is Drew, but I don't remember his last name), "Hey, try not to get hurt over here," I guess making a joke. Apparently, that did not sit well with that guy because he and second baseman Judah Wilbur began yelling at Mitch about how they'd been treated. I would later learn that when Mitch was first driving the cart onto the field, Drew had asked him if they could get someone to rake the first base area to smooth it out, and after the Zooperstars were done with their act for that inning, Mitch said what he said, so that cleared that up for me because at first I thought Drew was just being irrational. I did ask him what was so wrong, and he began to tell me some of the drama they had faced all season, but after a minute or so, he said he didn't want to talk to me about it since he liked me and didn't want to get me in any trouble, which I understood. It probably was the right thing to do.

The yelling later carried over to Dane, the Tommyknockers' GM, so much so that Mitch told us after the game that he might tell the Tommyknockers they were done for the season. The players met with Dane today about wanting to make admission free for the rest of the season. I believe they told Dane it was because they wanted to give something back to the city of Butte, but I think the reality was they didn't want him to make any more money off of him. At first, he agreed, but later in the day, he called off the remainder of their games this season so my partner and I would be there with nothing to do for four days.

Except Mitch told my partner that night we're going to Minot, ND, for the Sabre Dogs' last three games. I anticipated it would only be three instead of five because their last two games were supposed to be against the Tommyknockers, but obviously not anymore. The Minot team has already clinched, and the Sunfish, who was going to be the opposing team up there until more schedule changes resulting from the Tommyknockers and Sodbusters also calling it quits for the summer because of the lack of players still on the roster. So, I was hoping those three games would be easy. Unless the Sunfish decides to be done as well within the next 36 hours or so, then it will get even more interesting.

But actually, now we're in Gering, NE, after a ten-hour drive from Butte for a three-game series with the Fremont Moo, who are holding first place in the Clark Division by half a game at the time I write this, starting tomorrow (8/3). At the same time, the Big

Sticks and Spuds play three games in Caldwell before we have their last two games in Dickinson. Hopefully, they'll beat the Spuds twice in Caldwell, and the Spuds decide to call their season as well, so we don't have to call any more games after the third game here in Gering.

So, when you ask me how my summer went, this whole incident pretty much embodies it all as the climax of a crazy and unstable summer. There are five measly games left. Three here in Gering and two in Dickinson, unless the Big Sticks win two games and eliminate the Spuds, after which the Spuds decide not to travel thirteen hours across two states to play two games that don't matter. I honestly care more about those games than the ones I have here in Gering. However, I am glad that this means I will get to see every team in the Expedition League after all because I wasn't originally scheduled to see the Pioneers when I was in Crew A and Crew B, but now I will. I will have seen all twelve teams, and all but two of the home ballparks (Spearfish Sasquatch in South Dakota, the closest team to Mount Rushmore, and a home team I was scheduled to go to when in Crew A, and Hastings Sodbusters in Nebraska).

Not too much longer at all, but it seems so long sometimes. I just found out that the Big Sticks beat the Spuds today, so now the Big Sticks only need to win one more game against the Spuds, and the Lewis division is set. Gosh, I hope they do it tomorrow so the Spuds have more time to realize that traveling thirteen hours through two states and some change for two games that don't matter isn't a practical idea, and they can go ahead and call their last few games, at least the last two in Dickinson. It makes too much sense not to happen, especially if the Big Sticks win tomorrow and the Spuds have the time to realize that, which is a tall order in this equation. Pray with me for that.

August 3

Today, I had a base game here in Gering, NE, where the Western Nebraska Pioneers hosted the Fremont Moo, and will for the next two games this series. I had a play at second base where the second baseman bobbled the ball while trying to turn a double play but grabbed the ball and threw it at the last second to get it out. I had firm and secure possession and a voluntary release, so it was good.

Later in the game, another play at second base was on a potential double play. The toss to the shortstop was good, and after he had it for a quick second, the ball went flying in the direction of where his throwing hand was, so I maintained the out and used the "transfer" mechanic to signal that the out still counted and that the ball came out on the transfer, not a bobbled ball. I'm getting better every day, I guess.

Yesterday, I said I was hoping that the Badlands Big Sticks would beat the Spuds to clinch the Lewis division in the second half, and that did indeed happen tonight. All I need now is for the Spuds to think better than to travel thirteen hours across two states to play two meaningless games. If that happens, and no other games are scheduled as replacements, which would be a ridiculous idea, then Tristyn and I would be finished after our game on Thursday. We would head to Dickinson, ND, on Friday because we would be going there anyway, plus Tristyn will start the postseason there. We will likely stop at Mount Rushmore and have that day, including Saturday, for ourselves. Tristyn would then take me to the Bismarck Airport, where my flight is on Sunday. Lord, if you're there, please enlighten the Spuds. Amen.

My Delta flight from Bismarck will first go to Minneapolis for a two-hour and forty-one-minute layover. Then, I'll go from Minneapolis to Atlanta, where my family will pick me up to drive me two more hours back home. It feels so close, but I still have at least two games left, one at each position. The Pioneers and Moo better be swinging tomorrow.

If you wouldn't mind praying for the Spuds to decide not to travel, I would greatly appreciate that. It makes too much sense not to happen, but sense isn't something this league is full of, as you've undoubtedly been able to see if you've been following my summer. That's a big reason why I'm more than ready to be back in the southeast or even in an airport. Once I get my bags checked in Bismarck, get through security, and find my gate, I'll finally find peace, knowing that all will be right again soon.

There are four (or hopefully two) measly games left, and only the first two here mean anything because the Moo is a half-a-game back of the Spearfish Sasquatch for the Clark Division second half, the only other postseason spot not determined. I'm hoping the Sasquatch will win so Tristyn's travels are shorter because Spearfish is much closer than Fremont. The four postseason teams would be Minot, ND; Dickinson, ND; Spearfish, SD, and Gering, NE. However, for personal reasons, I don't care who wins that spot, but I would like the Pioneers to win these next two games so that we only have to play the top of the 9th instead of the whole inning. That would likely result in Spearfish winning that spot, especially if more teams decide not to play anymore or not travel. As long as my last game is Thursday, I'm good.

August 7

I haven't written for a few days, but now I'm in Dickinson for the final two games this season, so I'll try to sum up how calling the second and third Pioneers games were.

In the plate game, I had two ejections. Tristyn tossed the Pios assistant, and I tossed their manager for mocking me after giving him a warning. I had a good game, but the fans there are the worst in the league. That was apparent the next day when, before the game, the owner of the team was talking trash about over the walkie-talkies the interns had, and after the game, the fans were yelling at us through the door of our "dressing room," which was just their field equipment shed and ticket booth in one. The Pios are scheduled to host the first round of the postseason, but I say take them out and just put the Moo and Sasquatch in. Even if that doesn't happen, they have to deal with the biggest rule nazi in the league, Matt Beaver. Good luck with that.

Earlier in the summer, I kept a baseball from my plate game on Father's Day and sent it to my dad. I kept one from the Fourth of July when I also had the plate and sent it to my Pop. Yesterday, I had the thought to keep a baseball from that plate game since it was my last "regular" one (Yesterday was my dad's birthday) and send it, along with a letter, to my best friend Tucker, who's in college right now in Bowling Green, OH because that's where he was accepted to play football. I first met him when I joined the school baseball team in eighth grade. Even though Tucker is a year younger than me, because the school combined the seventh grade and eighth graders onto the same team, he was on that team as well. He would often approach me and ask me stuff to try to get to know me, but I wasn't comfortable since I was in an unfamiliar setting, so I tried to give very short answers and hoped he'd move along. In my head, I would want him to go away and leave me alone, but now I'm glad he didn't, since we've been friends ever since. As the years have passed and I've gotten more comfortable socially, we've gotten closer. So it sucks with him being gone for so long during the year, but me being very preoccupied this summer myself has shifted my attention, so I haven't noticed. Still, it's been a long time since I've seen him, and I haven't gotten to talk to him much this summer because sometimes our time doesn't line up, but I felt like I wanted to send him a baseball, so I did.

Here in Dickinson, the Big Sticks GM isn't here, but they're not missing a beat as everything is still running smoothly. I had a good plate game last night, although it was packed with eventful stuff, such as my first triple play and a very close fair/foul call, all while wearing my blue mask pads since my dad's birthday was yesterday. It was harder to breathe, but I made it through. And that's all I have to do today on the bases, and the storm will finally be over.

It was kind of nice to see the Spuds again. The manager they began the season with was promoted to GM, but he was the manager yesterday. I guess since it's the last two games, he decided to get back to the helm and have some fun.

August 8

Last night's game wasn't too bad. The Spuds manager came out to ask me about a judgment call at first, but to no avail. Later in the game, both teams started making silly substitutions, including a Spuds position player throwing emphus pitches. It almost felt like a weight was lifted once the final out was recorded.

I head home today on my mother's birthday, and I'm writing this as I'm in the car on the way to Bismarck Airport. I'll set my stuff down outside when I get home tonight because we don't want to bring potential bedbugs into the house.

So, the season is over (except for the postseason, which Tristyn will be working). I hope y'all have enjoyed reading about this crazy summer more than I enjoyed being in it. I'll be starting another semester of college at Chattahoochee Valley Community College in a couple of weeks, and that will be the most welcome first day of school I'll have ever had. I hope all is well back home or wherever you are, and I'm looking forward to returning there this evening.

I have less than an hour before I'll be at the airport, so once I get through there, it should be smooth sailing "or flying."

EJECTION REPORTS

May 26 - Wolfe Field: Caldwell, Idaho
Mining City Tommyknockers vs. Canyon County Spuds

At the bottom of the 6th inning, after calling strike 3, Sean Walsh (Spuds manager) took a few steps in my direction from the 3rd base coaches box and criticized my strike zone. Remembering that he had been chirping throughout the game, I ejected him. Afterward, he jogged to me and blamed his ejection on me supposedly not being able to call pitches correctly and went on about it being a one-run game (At the time, it was actually four runs, but he also put that on me). My partner, Jake Al-Mazroa, soon came over, and Sean said to him, "I don't know why you're coming over here. Both of you need to figure it out." He then left the playing field.

June 4 - Mike Lansing Field: Casper, Wyoming
Souris Valley Sabre Dogs vs. Casper Horseheads

At the top of 7th, after a wild pitch that allowed the Sabre Dogs runner to score from third base, Kyle Pearson (Horseheads manager) approached me behind the plate and violently shouted, "There's no way." After just a few seconds of what I felt was him showing me up, I ejected him. Pearson continued to yell and spit in my face, saying that I didn't know what I was doing and that I was "f**king 12 years old out here." My partner, Jake Al-Mazroa, soon came forth and got Pearson to head away from the playing field, which Pearson left afterward.

June 12 - Karras Park- Augustana University: Sioux Falls, South Dakota
Souris Valley Sabre Dogs vs Sioux Falls Sunfish

At the top of 6th, after a foul ball that struck the Sunfish catcher, I paused to give the catcher time to recuperate. However, Sunfish manager Walker Bullington screamed from their dugout that I should've gone out to the mound and "figured it out!" I said, "That's enough," because by then, the catcher was fine, and it was time to keep the game moving. Bullington continued without regard for my warning after giving it, so I called time and removed him from the game. My partner Tristyn Jones went over to the Sunfish dugout to de-escalate the situation, after which Bullington left the dugout.

June 20 - Merchants Park: Carroll, Iowa
Wheat City Whiskey Jacks vs. Sioux Falls Sunfish; Carroll, Iowa

At the bottom of 7th, the Whiskey Jacks assistant coach, Mark Reardanz, yelled that they were changing pitchers because of me and used his hands and body to show me the correct strike zone. I removed him from the game during his tirade. He continued to yell about the strike zone. I did not respond. He finally left the field.

July 6 - Astoria Field: Dakota Bank and Trust Ballpark in Dickinson, North Dakota
Souris Valley Sabre Dogs vs. Badlands Big Sticks

At the top of 5th, following a safe call at third base, Big Sticks manager Billy Tomblin left the dugout to discuss the call with me. That went on for a few moments, and then he began to retreat towards the dugout. While heading toward the dugout, he continued yelling at me. I removed Tomblin from the game. He then returned to my position in the infield to argue his removal. I continued explaining what I already had. My partner Tristyn Jones, who made his way toward me as Tomblin was after his removal, told him that he had to leave. He left the field.

July 17 - Kraft Field: Grand Forks, North Dakota
Pierre Trappers vs. Wheat City Whiskey Jacks

At the top of the 4th inning, I called Trappers runner Richard Williams (jersey number 1) out at 3rd base. He reacted negatively to the call, saying, "You gotta be blind." I removed Williams from the game. He soon left the field.

After the bottom of the 6th inning, Trappers pitcher Parker Lewis (Jersey number 26) walked off the field after the third out. He continuously yelled at me to "Figure it out" and soon said, "Figure it the f*** out!" I removed Lewis from the game. He looked back and said more before eventually leaving the field.

July 25- 3 Legends Field: Butte, Montana
Pierre Trappers vs. Mining City Tommyknockers

In the bottom of the 7th, after a check-swing call in which I ruled that the Tommyknockers hitter went around on, the Tommyknockers dugout reacted, including Tommyknockers assistant coach Jacob Schubert, who said something personal, to the extent of me not being able to do my job. I removed Schubert from the game. He continued yelling, and so did I, with us converging within the infield. The situation died down, and Schubert left the playing field.

In the bottom of the 7th, after a pitch, Tommyknockers hitter Judah Wilbur, number 29, yelled in my direction. It seemed to me that he was still upset about the previous call. I removed Wilbur from the game. He reacted and went back to the Tommyknockers dugout. He remained there for a few moments but eventually left the playing field.

July 28 - Astoria Field at Dakota Bank and Trust Ballpark in Dickinson, North Dakota
Mining City Tommyknockers vs. Badlands Big Sticks

In the bottom of the 4th inning, after a pitch I called a ball, Tommyknockers' reserve player Jeremy Husband yelled, "Figure it out" multiple times from the dugout. I went over and warned their dugout. He responded by saying, "That's bad." I removed him from the game. He soon gathered his stuff and left the playing field.

August 4 -Oregon Trail Park Stadium: Gering, Nebraska
Fremont Moo vs. Western Nebraska Pioneers

At the top of the 3rd, after a pitch, I called a ball, Pioneers manager Antonio Garcia was yelling about the pitch. I give him a warning. He mocks me with a sarcastic facial expression as if to sarcastically say that he's intimidated. I removed him from the game. He comes out to argue his ejection. He soon walks back to the dugout to collect his things. He left the playing field.

CHARACTER LIST
Samuel Barrett: Me

Umpire School (Status in 2021)
Hunter Wendelstedt: Owner/Operator of the school, MLB Umpire #21

Jerry Layne: Senior umpire in MLB after Joe West's retirement, MLB Umpire #24

Jansen Visconti: MLB Umpire #52

Junior Valentine: Head classroom instructor, MLB call-up Umpire #115

Other Instructors:
Ben Engstrand
Tom Hanahan
Reed Basner
Jake Bruner
Tom Fornarola
James Jean
Matt Carlyon

Peers:
Xavier Wood: From Texas, roommate, crew mate, nicknamed "Morning Wood" and "DACA"

Jeff Wallace: From New York, old (Was born during Eisenhower administration), crew mate, took pictures and sent them to everyone in an email

Mike MacStudy: Crewmate, nicknamed "MacSexy," progressively shaved off parts of his facial hair as the month went along

Matt Beaver: Crewmate

Jordan Smart: Crewmate, second-year student

Frank Barlow: Crewmate during the second half of school

Frank Jones: Roommate for the last couple of days of school

Derek Stevenson: From Atlanta, Georgia, black Republican, aspiring ACC umpire

Alex Schumaker: From Salisbury, North Carolina, known for Southern accent

Kolten Black: From Pittsburgh, Pennsylvania, nicknamed "Pete Davidson" due to his resemblance to the actor

Marv Gomez: resembles a little guy in the Black People Song

Ryan Haswell: He said he was needed back at the North Pole during Top Tens due to his apparent elf-like appearance.
Jack Wason (Pronounced like "Watson" without the T).

Butch Davis: From Idaho, saw me umpire my first games in

UMPIRE DIARY

Caldwell, Idaho.

John Poulin: Pastor, nicknamed "John the Baptist" had my first live inning with him, led us in prayer beforehand

Thomas Pruitt: Crewmate, from Alabama, left after the first week due to injury

Perry Schwartz
ArRee Bateman
Reggie Drummer
Garrett Forsythe
Asa Droddy
Larry Garcia
Romeo Garcia (No relation w/ Larry)
David Jamksi
Shawn McKinney
Sam Carray
Payton Oltmann
George Daubner
Scott Anderson
Micah Holman
Garrett Balmer
Keith Keyser
Spencer Kim
Will Bennett
Brian Lambe
Chad Little
Hayden Braack
Zach Lutz

SAMUEL BARRETT

Travis Brewer
Eddie Britt
Ryne Manka
Tyler Bryan
Steve Moore
Jason Coleman
Michael Reilly
Michael Rosales
Brandon Francisco
Jason Sperry
Ty Steele
Adrian Gonzales
Gabriel Torres
Troy Grimes
Jacob Waldrop
Nathan Hall
Cameron Bartley
Garrett Webster
Matt Youkhanna

Expedition League
League Office
Steve Wagner: President
Mitch Messer: Vice President
Connie Wagner: Covered finances

Umpire Roster:
Jake Al-Mazroa: My first partner, left mid-season due to knee injury

Connor Crowell: Left early in the season when a Northwoods League position opened for him

Tristyn Jones: Crowell's first partner, my second partner and partner for majority of season

Alex Schumaker: Friend from umpire school

Chad Williams: Schumaker's first partner, left early in the season due to family
Garrett Forsythe: Friend from umpire school

Asa Droddy: Friend from umpire school, Forsythe's partner
Anthony Atkinson

George Tyree: Atkinson's partner

Paul Settecase: Rarely heard from

Tony Archina: Settecase's partner, rarely heard from

Matt Beaver: Schumaker's second partner, friend from umpire school

Notable Team Personnel
Canyon County Spuds:

Sean Walsh: Manager, General Manager later in the season

Mining City Tommyknockers:

Tom Carty: Manager, I never saw him since he joined the team late and left the team before I had them again

Jason Schubert: Assistant Coach

Judah Wilbur: MIF, #29

Miles Hartsfield: IF, #3, I saw him again at a Georgia Southwestern State University exhibition game a year later

Dane Wagner: General Manager, son of league president
Dave Sheffield: Co owner w/ Dane, man who would have led to more sustainability and success with the team

Casper Horseheads:
Kyle Pearson: Manager

Souris Valley Sabre Dogs:
Alex Miklos: Manager
Beau Brewer: 1B, #18

Pierre Trappers:
Kelcy Nash: General manager
Monterio May: Manager
Jamie Habeger: Assistant Coach
Caiden Cardoso: P/1B, #33
Sioux Falls Sunfish:

Nick Moen, General Manager
Walker Bullington: Manager, from Mobile AL
Declan Beers: C, #3, catcher who was hit by the foul ball when
Bullington wasn't happy with how I gave Beers time to recover

Badlands Big Sticks:
Jason Watson: General manager
Billy Tomblin: Manager

Wheat City Whiskey Jacks:
Robby Laughlin: Manager
Mark Reardanz: Pitching coach
Nolan Lingley: #3, Final out of the no-hitter the Trappers threw
against the Whiskey Jacks
Nolan Drill: #7, It took me a good portion of the season to
decipher one of the team's chants was "Drill" for this guy
Keenan O'Brien: C, #9, my favorite of the Whiskey Jacks catchers,
but he didn't catch much

Zoe Hicks: IF/DH, #14, only girl player in the league that summer

Jake Hjelle (Pronounced like "Jelly"): 1B/DH, #32, good power
hitter, was one word away from being ejected by Tristyn after a
pickoff attempt in Pierre

Other Supporting Cast

Terry Boyer: Tenth and twelfth-grade science teacher, taught a
lot of life lessons in class that I still look back at and appreciate,
even when few others at the school did

SAMUEL BARRETT

Taylor Duncan: CEO, operator, and founder of Alternative Baseball, has provided opportunities to others like me, similar to the opportunity I had in eighth grade when I joined the baseball team, and it helped me grow socially

Fred Remick: Professional therapist/counselor I went to see starting in 2020 when things were rough. In 2022, he took a job at Fort Benning (Now Fort Moore), so I haven't been able to see him since, but he gave me someone I felt comfortable thinking out loud with

Tucker Melton: A year, a month, and three days younger than me, but one of the three best friends I've ever had and the one I've had the longest. The ways he helped me grow out of my social bubble added to my confidence that built up over time and eventually allowed me to leave home for umpire school, and then the Expedition League

Matt Law: Former pastor of my age's church group until he took a job north of Atlanta. I still keep in touch with him and have Bible Study with him on a weekly basis

Grandpa: My maternal grandfather, the most likely genetic source of my often sarcastic and what many people call "smart" remarks and personality, a family member I've always been very close with

This section also serves as more acknowledgments, as all these people made my umpire school experience and Expedition League experience what it was, from the positives that I enjoyed to the negatives that I learned from.

Q&A

As I was deciding to write this book, I remembered more and more that not many people hear from baseball umpires, whether it be by choice or not having the opportunity. Many people have questions about umpires or their procedures. Since ignorance is not bliss and there are only easy answers to those who are uninformed, I feel that answering some of the burning questions about baseball from the official's perspective would be beneficial to help bridge the gap between umpires and those in baseball who aren't umpires. From the outside looking in, some things can look so simple, but once you learn the rules, procedures, and feelings of being in the game, they don't seem so simple anymore. Perhaps I can help form the bridge of understanding here with this Q&A section.

Disclaimer: This section is only for those who are open-minded and willing to learn. If you don't take criticism well or are so steadfast in what you believe to be true from the outside that you won't even entertain input from someone who has been there, you don't deserve the insights I'm about to give.

We know power-five Division One umpires and big league umpires are treated well. We also know umpires in Little League through low-level D1 are treated horribly in terms of pay, changing areas, etc. How can those umpires with the power, status, knowledge, and resources help form a union or assist us in getting fair treatment that we deserve? Or how can

*the MLB umpires help amateur-level umpires form a union?
-Adam Luck, a friend from my second time through umpire
school*

I've seen major college umpire dressing rooms,
professional dressing rooms, and, of course, high school and travel
dressing rooms. As for those below the division one level, those
dressing rooms can vary from being air-conditioned lounges with
tables, chairs, and perhaps a few lockers to wooden sheds that are
used for storage every day of the year except baseball game days,
and of course the center tower in the middle of a field complex
(What I like to call "Ring around the rosie fields"). To be fair, many
schools simply aren't in good enough financial positions to
provide lavish quarters, and if they do, they will supply them to
their players first since that's who they're investing the most time
and money into. But I think it's reasonable to infer that if the
umpires don't have a really nice dressing room, the players'
clubhouse likely isn't all that great either, if it exists at all, so it's
not like teams are intentionally being unkind to umpires in this
regard.

As for pay, the man who asked this question has done all
his research and can tell you that perfect game, for example, could
double umpire pay and still make bank and a half. In Alabama,
every school I've heard discuss potential umpire shortages has
agreed to pay more, but the state doesn't allow it without a state-
wide change to the pay guide. At first, that sounds like the state is
the problem, but they likely don't allow schools to pay more as
they please to prevent bribery. See, things often have more
moving parts than you initially think.

I've discussed a solution to umpire shortages on family friend

Brian Hickman's podcast Under The Purg, where I said, "If you're not on the field, keep your mouth shut." However, I'm aware that that is a very simplified solution that wouldn't just happen by waving a magic wand, so here are a few solutions to the umpire shortage:

1. **Remember the GAME.**
   That's what baseball is; a game. Some people say this about youth sports and say it should be fun at that level, which is true. But that should be the case at every level, including the major professional level. I don't care how much someone is getting paid, how much someone bet on a game, how much someone paid to be there, or anything else-it's still a game at the end of the day. It doesn't determine how good of a person you are, nor will God consider it when your Judgement Day comes. I realize many people have been brainwashed into believing that sport is so important, and then they do the same damage to their children, but what I'm saying is the truth, and you know it's true, but you must allow your mind to believe it again.

2. **Raise children right.**
   This goes with the above point. Suppose you teach your kids that the sport is so valuable in the grand scheme of life and that they must succeed at it to feel worthy. In that case, they will be more likely to anger easily when something doesn't go their way, such as if an umpire rules against them, and then they're more likely to be penalized for their actions. If it helps, try seeing it from my perspective: my

friend Tucker started playing baseball when he was four years old, so he was active and social. When I was four, my family was putting me through early intervention with the hopes that it would develop me enough that I could start kindergarten on time. No matter how bad you think your current situation is, someone has it worse, particularly if your problem is a 0-3 day. I'd take that over being scolded by a teacher because I didn't know how to wash my hands.

3. **Stiffer penalties for abuse towards officials**.
This is a big one for me. Umpires aren't taught to be tough anymore. Today's prima donna players wouldn't last an inning on the same field as Al Barlick, Shag Crawford, Jocko Conlan, and Doug Harvey. The last good umpire like that in MLB is probably Jerry Layne, but Joe West is the best umpire, current or former, who's still alive. People didn't like him because he didn't give in like today's umpires do. I'm sorry, but watching Erik Bacchus getting chewed out by David Ross and Bacchus just standing there and doing nothing embarrassed me for him. No one should be treated like that, but I see it at every level today because they're being taught that way. If you don't give someone five warnings, your assigner won't back you up in an ejection. Kids these days need toughness to bend them into shape. Team personnel feel way too bold, and the umpires don't, which are two big ingredients for lawlessness. That happened in the summer of 2020 when many city officials in big cities weren't tough on crime. Property was destroyed, innocent people were harassed, and this often went unpunished due to lawyers, judges, and prosecutors

who simply let the perpetrators out of jail soon without punishment. And sometimes a warning won't cut it, so you have to eject right away, and umpire school teaches that. Unfortunately, I've had assigners who are too scared to do that and want to accommodate people who don't deserve to be accommodated. How do you fix all this? Motivate umpires and make them feel powerful. I like to tell umpires it is their game; they call it their way, and the only rule in the book you actually have to know is 8.01 (d-e).

The rest are technically just conveniences. Yes, you teach standard situation protocol, but then you abide by it, which, for some reason, when I do, people have an issue with it. Penalties for ejections? Similar to steroids, the first offense entails a remainder of season suspension. The second offense incurs suspension for the remainder of the season and the next whole season. A third offense means that you would be banned for life. Harsh? Yes, and you'd never have another problem. Those who disagree with what I'm saying are more than likely the soft people I'm referring to. If you think you're right, publish a book rebutting me. This doesn't have to be the way it is, but I think starting off this way until people get the message shouldn't be left off the table.

Unfortunately, today's big league umpires live too lavishly to desire to be concerned with helping officials in lower levels get these benefits. Still, each level has someone like me who doesn't stand for bullcrap. Whoever you are out there, for things to be made better, you have to be the one. Don't put up with any injustice or disrespect-you're likely doing a great job as it is. Teach your ways to other umpires, and never let another umpire backtrack anything you do. If they try, threaten to leave. If we want things to improve for umpires, there can be no room for indifference or flakiness. We must demand improvements and teach others how to treat us on a large scale. If not everyone does it, it won't catch on. A massive revolution must occur; I think a shortage would be a fantastic way to do it. Before long, all those brainwashing parents and brainwashed kids will be so desperate to get their sport back because they don't value truly important stuff in life that they will agree to literally anything. Make all your demands known, and don't give in until you have every last one of them. They WILL eventually give in. Today's players, coaches, parents, and fans won't be able to stand to go too long without their sport. They will have to give you everything if you persist.

Is being an umpire more or less challenging than you initially thought?
-DJ Rias, former high school baseball teammate

I didn't know what to think at first. Going into umpire school, I knew I didn't know how to call a game, but I was very confident that I would learn how to during the next month. As with any class, there were some things that I picked up on right away and some that I struggled with for a few weeks. A great thing that the instructors did was acknowledge that many people go to umpire school to start from scratch. So, they teach as if everyone is entirely new. Throughout the course, Jansen often told us at the podium at the end of the day, "Do not get discouraged." I suppose that sounds cliché, but I think it helped us; at least it did me. By the end of the course, I had gotten everything down, had gotten a job recommendation, and started my first season of high school ball a couple of weeks later.

Obviously, being at umpire school and being in a real game is different. So, are the games more challenging or easier than I expected? Since I based nearly everything I did off of umpire school for that first year, the same answer applies here: I didn't know what it would be like. Sometimes, at umpire school, it seems intimidating, but as I've grown and gotten more games, among them higher-level games, I rarely get nervous on the field, and I feel confident in every mechanic and decision I make. So, I didn't have an initial expectation, but I've settled in very nicely.

What is your favorite part about doing it?
-DJ Rias

I would say my favorite aspects are two broad things:

1. I like to view baseball as a sport, not a game, and definitely not as a business or investment, but as an art. If you're wondering what I mean by "baseball as an art," it's not hard to see: the sound of wooden bats not just when they hit a baseball, but when they're being organized in the bat rack, the clear-cut lines in the grass before the game, the chalk lines and white plate before hitters kick it all away with needless digging (Don't you hate it when guys do that?), seeing the colors of the team uniforms and identities pop, especially if the teams have clearly distinct color schemes—no similar colors like navy vs. blue, or teams with the same colors. I like it when teams look entirely different. Smelling something good grilling or frying, hearing how loud the

crowd can get upon a positive event for the team they came to see, and even how I look on the field. I crease the front of my cap in the same manner many pros do (That's what that bend in the top of the hat is if you ever notice it). I roughly keep the number of baseballs in each ball bag, even if I can, to make sure each side looks the same. I clean my shoes before every game and hustle. Many older umpires below the college level don't hustle, but I do, and that earns me a lot of compliments, which I tend to get a lot of for different reasons. I'll take them.

2. Even though I complained about many aspects of the Expedition League, I got to see the inside of the South Dakota State Capitol (I haven't seen any other states, not even Alabama's), the city of Sioux Falls. I can now join my father in saying I've been to Iowa. I saw the Roger Maris museum and his grave both in Fargo, an American Association independent professional game. I was an hour south of Canada in Minot. I saw an All-Star Game for the first time, Old Faithful erupting at Yellowstone National Park, Our Lady of the Rockies in the backdrop of a field, the Badlands, and Scotts Bluff National Monument. We passed right by the geographic center of the entire US, as well as Grand Teton National Park, some picturesque landscapes while traveling from city to city, and even some things in Texas since my dad took me out there so I could learn to fly. As a result, I saw the Alamo, ate on the riverwalk in San Antonio with a real Mariachi band in the background, and I saw the Astrodome. The new places I've visited because of the simple decision to start umpiring games surpass anything else I've ever done or experienced. If I were forced to leave the southeast US, Sioux Falls would be one of my

first options for moving. Just as well, I can confidently say there are some places I would NOT recommend. Seeing some of this great nation has made me curious to see more. I've always wanted to visit Washington, D.C., and see all those monuments, memorials, and bureaucratic buildings. Now, I feel it is possible to see so many physical marvels that the United States offers, which has increased my desire to see them. Places such as the Statue of Liberty, Empire State Building, Trump Tower, and 9/11 Memorial in New York City; the Hollywood Sign, the streets of Hollywood and Sunset Boulevards and Vine Street (As opposed to seeing just the signs for them and the restaurant Hollywood and Vine at Disney World's Hollywood Studios) in Los Angeles, and other landmarks in Chicago, San Francisco, Dallas, and other American cities are things that have been shown to me in photos since I was a young child. My curiosity for them has never wavered, and thanks to my travels in the EL, they have intensified. Perhaps someday, I'll decide that I'm in a position where I could go to one of these American marvels. The inner kid in me can just stand in wonder that this city, statue, or building that I had only ever seen in photos or heard about exists. Here I am, standing right by it, almost feeling that I do not deserve to be in the presence of such an icon. The destinations that games have taken me to sometimes make the entire endeavor worthwhile just for that.

Is it hard staying unbiased during a game?
-DJ Rias

For the most part, a person's personal bias before becoming an umpire goes away rather quickly as they learn to call a game. There are so many things that officials must have on their minds at any given time that there isn't any room for choosing a team to win. So those conspiracy theories about officials trying to bend a game towards one side are unfounded and only suggested by those without appropriate expertise and experience.

That said, there can be times when an umpire will have an ideal situation in mind and hope it happens. For example, if the home team is winning by a run in the top of the ninth, they likely want the pitching and defense to ensure the hitting doesn't do anything so the game can end without going to the bottom half of the inning. If a game is tied in the bottom half, they likely want the hitting to score this half-inning, so there are no extra innings. If there is a run rule for this game, and it's in effect, but they have to let the losing team get one more half-inning at-bat, then we don't really want the losing team to score. If the home team is only a couple of runs away from enacting the run rule in the bottom half of an inning where a run rule takes effect, we may want the home team to score those runs so the game can end. And, of course, if one team is behaving well and one is severely misbehaving, guess who's getting the benefit of the doubt on close plays?

Of course, we don't act on these thoughts (At least not typically), but we can't help but see these things as they wander into our heads. I have never changed how I've called a game just so one team would get run-ruled or so a game would end since I believe that would be making the game unfair, and the whole point of me being there is to keep the game fair (which is not the same as equal, mind you). Sometimes fair is a team getting blown out and having four players ejected because they're not good on the field or with their attitudes. If that doesn't happen to the other team, then sure, it's not equal, but it is fair.

At this point, I don't have any trouble with internal bias. However, I still have some names of specific guys on different teams that I keep in mind, so I know not to give them extra leeway next time I have them in a game. Umpires have been getting even since the beginning, and sometimes, if you can do that during a game rather than eject (If you don't have to eject, that is), then you've won. Of course, umpires always win since they're the one team on the field that never loses. We go out there having already won, but any slick moves we can pull off to effectively manage the game always help.

1. What do you think of the current rules?
2. Are there any rules you would change currently?
3. What does an average gameday look like for you?
4. What are the three keys to being a good umpire?
-Noah Shelton, a family friend and broadcaster for Columbus summer teams in 2023

1. Baseball rules are complicated. That's just one of the many facts of life. If you don't think they are, look at the Official Baseball Rules and study them. There are so many twisted things in there that it's no wonder most people have to go to umpire school at least twice before

getting placed in pro ball. However, every rule is either to keep the game what it is or because something crazy happened that was not covered in the regulations, and the rules committee had to add or change something to cover it. As I've mentioned before, that can even happen at umpire school.

2. I suppose I would be okay with a computer calling the strike zone. That would allow me to not put on all the equipment and stand to the side when I have my plate assignments because the computer would do everything. They should have the count shown on the scoreboard, and that's how people would know what a pitch is. I think having this system could, and should, revolutionize umpire positioning. You would only need an umpire at the plate for plays there, so umpire committees could devise their rotation sequences, which would be the case when needed. In the two-umpire system, instead of one umpire behind the plate and another at "A" position (behind first base on the foul side of the line), the plate guy could shift over to "D" (same as "A," but on the third base side) so he could call fair-foul decisions down the left field line. On a base hit, the now third base umpire would rotate towards second base just as the third base guy does in the three-umpire system. With runners on base, however, you would need that "plate umpire" to position somewhere by home plate so they could rule on fair/foul decisions since the base umpire would still be inside the infield. For the three-umpire system, have an umpire at each base, and there you go. We could develop rotations to have a guy at home in case a decision needs to be

made. Perhaps working the plate would become the new "rocking chair" position, which is the name currently given to the third base umpire in a four-umpire system due to its relative lack of action and responsibility.

3. Most of my games are evening or night games, so until mid-afternoon, I do what I please, although that could consist of other responsibilities I need to accommodate. My high school games are over thirty minutes away because I'm in the Alex City Association, and they're in a different time zone. I've always been taught to get to the game site an hour before, so that's what I do, even though at the high school level, no one else I know of does that unless it's for a postseason game. I calculate the time needed to get to the field an hour before the first pitch. I leave at that time, and the first thing I do when I get to the field is put my umpire bag in our dressing room and go walk the field. This does two things: it allows me to get a look at the field I will be calling on that day so I can see where the fences are tight, where there are holes, and any concerning things that I may need to bring up at the plate meeting. This is the main reason for walking the field. It also shows everyone that I am there early and that I care about this game. I'm looking at the field, so I know how to best officiate on it. What's better, I don't do it as an act-I do it as a graduate and therefore a representative of the teachings of the Wendelstedt Umpire School. That's what they teach, and I do it. Sometimes, I'll go places, and the coaches, and sometimes players, will recognize

me when I'm out there, and even tell me they're glad I have their game because they know how well I will call it. From there, I return to the dressing room and wait for my partner to get there. We discuss the game if needed, and around ten minutes before the first pitch, we head for home plate for the plate meeting, the national anthem if that will be played or performed, and, of course, the game.

Once the game(s) are over, I get undressed, head home, and put my hurting feet into bed.

4. I suppose I could give a few good guidelines that umpires should follow, but I believe the *Official Baseball Rules* do this well enough in the "General Instructions to Umpires," so I think now would be a good time to present what Junior says is his favorite part of the rulebook:

- *Umpires on the field should not indulge in conversation with players. Keep out of the coaching box, and do not talk to the coach on duty.*

- *Keep your uniform in good condition. Be active and alert on the field.*

- *Always be courteous to Club officials; avoid visiting Club offices and thoughtless familiarity with officers or employees of contesting Clubs.*

- *When you enter a ballpark, your sole duty is to umpire a ball game to represent baseball.*

- *Do not allow criticism to keep you from studying bad situations that may lead to protested games. Carry your rule book. It is better to consult the rules and hold up the game for ten minutes to decide a knotty problem than to have a game thrown out on protest and replayed.*

- *Keep the game moving. The energetic and earnest work of the umpires often helps a ball game.*

- *You are the only official representative of baseball on the ball field. It is often a trying position that requires much patience and good judgment, but do not forget that keeping your temper and self-control is essential in working out of a bad situation.*

- *You will undoubtedly make mistakes, but never attempt to "even up" after making one. Make all decisions as you see them and forget which is the home or visiting Club.*

- *Keep your eye everlastingly on the ball while it is in play. It is more vital to know where a fly ball fell or a thrown ball finished up than whether or not a runner missed a base. Do not call the plays too quickly or turn away too fast when a fielder is throwing to complete a double play. Watch out for dropped balls after you have called a man out.*

- *Do not come running with your arm up or down, denoting "out" or "safe." Wait until the play is completed before making any arm motion.*

- *Each umpire team should work out a simple set of signals so the proper umpire can always right a manifestly wrong decision when convinced he has made an error. If you are sure you got the play correctly, do not be stampeded by players' appeals to "ask the other man." If you are not sure, ask one of your associates. Do not carry this to extremes; be alert and get your own plays. But remember! The first requisite is to make decisions correctly. If in doubt, don't hesitate to consult your associate. Umpire dignity is important but never as important as "being right."*

- *The most important rule for umpires is always "BE IN POSITION TO SEE EVERY PLAY." Even though your decision may be 100% right, players still question it if they feel you were not in a spot to see the play clearly and definitely.*

- *Finally, be courteous, impartial, and firm, and command respect from all.*

CONCLUSION (2024)

It's now been two years since the events of this book took place. During my time in the Expedition League, I would not have imagined that I would look back at those times favorably one day. Writing this book allowed me to revisit those blog posts. I can now view them and the experiences they documented from the outside looking in. In doing so, I gained a new perspective.

I've always been glad I went to umpire school, but it took longer for me to feel the same about going to the Expedition League. In *Ball Four*, Jim Bouton hit the literary jackpot by being around a team of misfits, the Seattle Pilots, that only survived one season. Similarly, I just happened to be placed into a league that, due to its ineptitude, did not last. Perhaps someone in the future will wonder about the Expedition League. What was it like? What happened to it? Hopefully, they will find this book. If you are that person, I hope I have satisfied your curiosity.

As time goes by, change is inevitable. The Wendelstedt Umpire School was in danger of going under due to MLB changing its umpire recruitment processes. Fortunately, it still lives on in the same capacity that it always has, which I'm happy to hear. I'm not in professional baseball, but some of my old classmates are, including Frank Jones, Perry Schwartz, Travis Brewer, Sam Carray, and Jack Wason. I've even heard that Wason is now an instructor at the school. One of the instructors, Tom Hanahan, has been officiating fill-in games at the Major League level. Junior began his first season full-time in 2023, along with Erich Bacchus and Malachi Moore. The latter two were instructors during my second time through the school.

The Expedition League lost seven teams a few months after the season ended to form a new league: the Independence League. That left four teams in the EL: the Souris Valley Sabre Dogs, Pierre Trappers, Sioux Falls Sunfish, and Wheat City Whiskey Jacks. Steve Wagner brought breach of contract suits against the departing teams, but his efforts failed. The latter two teams seemed to disappear, while the Sabre Dogs and Trappers were joined by two new teams, the Red River Pilots and North Iowa Ragin' Roosters, for the 2022 season. Halfway through the season, those two teams dropped out, leaving the Sabre Dogs and Trappers. The league decided to have them play a best-of-five championship round. The Dogs won, giving them two EL championships in a row. They also went down in the books as the last league champions. While I know of no official statement, the league has folded for all practical purposes. President Steve Wagner landed as the commissioner of an independent football league. Either they didn't do their homework, or Steve felt he had learned enough from the Expedition League and is ready for a new venture. Apparently, after his appointment was announced, there was major backlash, and he was quickly relieved of his duties there.

Steve's son, Dane Wagner, the co-owner and GM of the Mining City Tommyknockers of Butte Montana, took most of the fallout from what developed with that team. A few weeks after Tristyn told me about the EL's version of Brexit, he was arrested for stealing a space heater from a mental health center. He was sleeping when the police found him and took him in for booking. I can't tell if it's ironic or merely coincidental that he was arrested and booked, considering he claimed to have written over one hundred best-selling books. Stephen King has only published sixty-three at, nearly twice Dane's age, so no one can be blamed for finding this hard to believe.

I returned to umpire school the following January. While I did keep up the blog during that time, I decided not to include it in this book since I didn't write as often. The experience the second time around wasn't quite as good. It was still fun, but there were many more people this time. Some of them were toxic as they spoiled the experience for others. I did see several people I remembered from the prior year, probably returning because of the tuition-free discount we were given. I also saw other familiar faces I knew from the Expedition League, such as Anthony Atkinson and David Shoptaw. David had been on the EL roster at one point but later left the league.

A lot has happened since umpire school ended. A week after I returned, I was heading home from a high school umpire meeting in Alexander City, AL, when a car in front of me blew a tire and quickly slowed down. Of course, I couldn't slow down in time, so my Herbie VW Beetle was gone for good. Later in the month, I learned the three-umpire system in Auburndale, FL, from United Umpires, the organization recently acquired by the Sunbelt Baseball League to provide umpires. The Sunbelt League is a summer league based out of Atlanta that had a team in Columbus, just ten minutes away from home for me. I managed to learn it well enough to get many Columbus games. I was relieved that I didn't have to go far away again to get decent baseball. In fact, Sunbelt games pay twenty dollars more than the Expedition League (SBL pays $100 per game vs. $80 from the EL).

In May of 2023, I got my Associate's Degree. There was a time when I wanted to finish a Bachelor's degree and then a Master's program, but over the past few months of studying current events and observing successful people who have significantly impacted the world, I've changed my mind. I've come to the realization that my time and money could be put to better use. I've decided not to invest more money on extra schooling, where the teachers (NOT "professors" - screw their arrogance!) are not particularly successful, and the money just flows to the athletic programs. In my opinion, colleges are already a corrupt system of injustice in this country. It's the largest mass indoctrination program and is never allowed to be even mentioned. There's no reason why a highly qualified student with a 3.5 GPA should get what amounts to "pocket change" to a small college while a moron who has never read a book in his life gets a full ride to a prestigious university. That's why I think very few, if any, college athletes should be considered to have earned a Bachelor's or Master's degree. It's an "athletic degree" and nothing more. Should I ever be elected president, that would be one of my top priorities. A better investment for that money would be learning about myself and how I could utilize my skills to serve as many people as possible. Why be in debt until I'm 50 when I can be financially independent when I'm 30, If not sooner?

I do have a college degree, for which I am grateful. Not many people have had to overcome the obstacles I've had to overcome at different points throughout my life, even enrolling in college, let alone finishing a degree plan. I take pride in having attained yet another accomplishment, and perhaps I can serve as an example to others who are on the spectrum or otherwise are in less-than-normal settings that they, too, can put together a life worth living.

There have been other changes since I first wrote these

excerpts: Tristyn moved from Palm Beach, Florida, to Henderson, Colorado, a few months after the Expedition League season ended. Last I checked, he still calls ball there. Tucker transferred to the University of West Alabama in Livingston, Alabama, which is much closer to home, so I got to see him a little more often than when he was in Ohio. Not only did he play more on their football team than with Bowling Green State's, he told me before his first season there that he was named their starting quarterback, so I got to go to some of his games. He returned home full-time to coach at Russell County High School, which was great since I knew he's always wanted to coach, plus, we could hang out even more often. Now, he is coaching at a school in Biloxi, Mississippi. Beau Brewer of the Souris Valley Sabre Dogs was drafted by the Yankees in 2022, and you can even see his stat line with the Sabre Dogs on his baseball-reference.com page.

I got to the second round of the postseason in the three years following the events of this book, and I advanced to the third round in 2024. I likely will continue to do so as long as I am umpiring. In October 2022, I was asked to officiate an exhibition game at Georgia Southwestern State University, where some players from the Expedition League were enrolled, including Miles Hartsfield from the Mining City Tommyknockers. I remember him because he was one of Tristyn's first two ejections of the season. He would occasionally coach first base and would try to urge me to call his teammates safe. The farthest I've been from Phenix City since the Expedition League is Disney World, while the farthest and most unfamiliar place is Chattanooga, Tennessee. It is a strange place, not only because the city parking is a disaster, but because the name sounds too silly to be proud of. "Hi, I live in Chattanooga, Tennessee!" I couldn't say that with a straight face. I couldn't even say I live in Tennessee with a straight face. It's kind of like Mississippi, but I can sort of make that one sound fine. With my dialect, I typically blend the two s-sounds and turn it into "MisSIPpi" (with emphasis on the middle syllable).

I'm 23 now as I write this, and putting this book together has created yet another unique experience for me to learn about myself. We all have something to offer the world that no one else can, but as you can imagine, that can be difficult to find, especially if one doesn't believe that to be the case. Writing this book has reminded me of the experiences no one else in my inner circle has seen. I've seen how I react in different situations and how that's changed over the years. I've seen how my brain thinks and how it's evolved...and sometimes how it's even stayed the same. Plenty of thoughts come into my head that very few others imagine. It's possible that many people contemplate an idea, but the only one you ever hear about is the one who actually takes the time and effort to turn it into a reality.

Even the fact that this book exists at all could serve as an example. If seeing the cover with my name on it can get someone's gears turning enough to see what they have to offer that others could use or enjoy, and then find a way to begin acting on it, I'll consider my time doing this to be well-spent. If reading this book can help someone who is going through a rough patch to take it one day at a time as I did, find at least one thing to savor every day, and power through because it will end, I'll be grateful that I was able to help someone. I may come back and read some of this book again to restore my confidence and remind myself that I can get through anything because I have done so before.

Everyone has something to bring to the table, and

someone is starving for it. The first day you genuinely believe that is the first day of the rest of your life.

BIOGRAPHY

I was born on November 3, 2000. I have a high-functioning form of autism known as Asperger's Syndrome, but thanks to access to excellent early intervention when I was still a toddler, it's not very noticeable and has not been since that time.

I graduated from Central High School in Phenix City, AL, in 2019 and Chattahoochee Valley Community College in 2023. I began my umpire career in 2021 by attending the Wendelstedt Umpire School in Ormond Beach, FL. After my recommendation for a league out of umpire school, I established myself with the Alexander City Baseball Umpires Association of the Alabama High School Athletic Association and have been calling games with them every spring since, even receiving postseason assignments in just my second, third, and fourth seasons due to my learning of the three-umpire system.

I continued to call summer college baseball, but closer to home. Since I experienced a lot in a short period of time, it is possible that I missed a story here and there, though I made my best effort to add everything whenever I remembered something during the writing stage. If you have any questions or comments, feel free to reach out to me via email: rsbarrett00@gmail.com

Made in the USA
Middletown, DE
01 September 2024

60265118R00104